CONFERRING WITH READERS

D1459914

CONFERRING WITH
READERS

Supporting Each Student's Growth and Independence

Gravity Goldberg • Jennifer Serravallo

HEINEMANN

PORTSMOUTH, NH

Heinemann

361 Hanover Street
Portsmouth, NH 03801–3912
www.heinemann.com

Offices and agents throughout the world

Library of Congress Cataloging-in-Publication Data
Serravallo, Jennifer
  Conferring with readers : supporting each student's growth and independence / Jennifer Serravallo and Gravity Goldberg.
    p. cm.
  Includes bibliographical references.
  ISBN-13: 978-0-325-01101-1
  ISBN-10: 0-325-01101-X
  1. Reading.   2. Books and reading.   I. Goldberg, Gravity.   II. Title.
  LB1050.G63 2007
  418'.4—dc22
                                                                                    2007027585

Editor: Kate Montgomery
Production service: Stephanie Lentz, Aptara
Production coordination: Sonja S. Chapman
Cover design: Joni Doherty
Interior photographs: Elizabeth White
Back cover photographs: Elizabeth White and Karen O'Maxfield
Compositor: Aptara
Manufacturing: Louise Richardson

Printed in the United States of America on acid-free paper
15 14 13 12   EB   7 8 9 10 11

To Our Students—
Past, Present, and Future

Contents

Acknowledgments

We cannot thank Lucy Calkins enough for her generosity—for sharing what she knows with us, for encouraging us to share our knowledge with others, and for challenging our thinking and pushing us to deepen our own understandings about teaching. It was Lucy who first gave us the idea and confidence to write this book. It is under her leadership that we have grown into the teachers and staff developers we are today. Lucy's work has influenced so much of the way we conceptualize teaching, learning, and assessment, and you will see her name all over this book. We feel so grateful to be a part of her organization, the Teachers College Reading and Writing Project (TCRWP).

We are continually inspired and motivated by Kathleen Tolan's passion for teaching reading. Kathleen leads the upper-grade reading work at the TCRWP, and we are influenced heavily by her brilliance. We feel so lucky to work with her. She is a mentor and a support to both of us.

Thank you to Kathy Collins for believing we had something to share and for reading a draft of this book. In addition, her work with young readers helped us build a strong foundation for what reading conferring looks like with primary-grade readers.

Every Thursday we gather with our colleagues at TCRWP to learn with and from each other. We meet in think tanks and study groups to learn more about balanced literacy and the teaching of reading and writing. Because of this amazing community of leaders and thinkers, this book is possible. To be part of this community has helped us in more ways than we can describe. Thanks to all of our colleagues, present and past, but especially Laurie Pessah, Amanda Hartman, Maggie Moon, Mary Ehrenworth, Mary Chiarella, and Joe Yukish for the work that they've done around reading and conferring, and the great knowledge they've shared with us.

The work in this book also stands on the shoulders of countless researchers and writers. Thanks to Katherine Bomer, Donna Santman, Marie Clay, Irene Fountas, Gay

Su Pinnell, Ellin Keene, and Richard Allington for all you've taught us through your books, workshops, and articles.

We'd like to thank the readers of drafts of this book: Jenny Bender, Lucy Calkins, Kathy Collins, Colleen Cruz, Kathleen Tolan, and Kimberly Quinlan. Their knowledge and advice gave us new perspectives and concrete ways to revise the book.

We are so thankful for Elizabeth White and Karen O'Maxfield's generosity. They donated their time to take the photos for this book. We are lucky to know such talented people.

We'd also like to thank the principals, teachers, and students with whom we work in the New York City public schools and in schools throughout the country. We'd especially like to thank P.S. 63, whose teachers' and students' faces grace the pages of this book, and P.S. 32, 63, 91, 102, 158, 182, 186, 242, and 277 for being guinea pigs for some of the work on these pages, offering feedback and suggestions when necessary. It was through teaching the content of this book to real teachers in real classrooms that we were able to go through several drafts and revisions.

Of course we would also like to thank Kate Montgomery, our editor. She served as a sounding board, critical reader, and cheerleader at times. Our final manuscript reflects her insightful suggestions and questions.

I (Jen) would like to thank the small but powerful education department at Vassar College. Robin Trainor, Chris Roellke, and Linda Cantor taught me that teaching is an art and a craft, and that it is activism. I am fueled every day by what I learned from Chris about urban education reform. Robin's and Linda's mentorship and support in my days as a student teacher are still as fresh in my mind as if they were yesterday. I would also like to thank my earliest teachers of conferring—Carl Anderson, Gaby Layden, and Amanda Hartman. I was lucky to learn from each of them in summer institutes at Teachers College and in year-long leadership groups when I was a classroom teacher. Jenny Bender, it's been great being writing buddies with you. Thank you to Colleen for your belief in me as a writer, and for your coaching and sound advice along the way. I appreciate your telling it to me straight, and I have tried to incorporate every bit of advice and critique you gave me (even the bit about dangling modifiers). You are my writing mentor and a valued friend. I would like to thank Jenifer D'Agosta for putting up with the computer on my lap for most of the winter and spring, and for supporting me in more ways than I have room to mention here. I am also grateful to my family. They have instilled in me the value of education, and I work every day to try to give other children the same experiences I have been afforded.

And I (Gravity) would like to thank Barbara McLaughlin for her mentorship and incredible knowledge of reading. Barbara taught me what it meant to study students' reading in deep and powerful ways, to look for strengths, and to support readers as they grow and blossom. I would also like to thank Kathleen Flannery, the finest principal I could have worked with. Thank you to Jon Roberts and Gary Goldberg-O'Maxfield for reading excerpts of the manuscript and offering constructive feedback that ultimately made the book better. I would like to thank my grandfather, Papa Joe, for teaching me that "much has been given to you and much is expected of you." I hope this book helps meet that expectation. Finally, I want to thank my mom, Josette. She has always believed in me and supported me, yet has the magical ability of not pushing too hard. She is my first and most inspiring teacher.

Authors' Note

We decided to write each chapter in the first person singular for readability purposes, but the reader should assume that each use of the word *I* really means *we*. We know how important it is for a reader to envision as she reads, so, in case you're wondering, Jen is the art pupil who regularly practices yoga and has a closet full of clothes that don't fit. Gravity is the runner, guitar student, and soccer player. This book was a true collaborative endeavor.

Foreword

When our students are finally, blissfully, engaged in Sustained, Silent Reading,—we never thought it would happen!—we at first want to simply lean back in our chairs, smile and congratulate ourselves. At long last, our kids are all on their way! After all, we know that consistent, engaged reading begets stronger and more thoughtful readers. Now, they are all reading; we've done our job.

But then we lean forward. Is that all? Our students are mostly able to choose books, and they now have time in school to read. Is that all they need? We start to feel uncomfortable. Okay, maybe that isn't all, but what more? What can we offer them that is worth disturbing the silence, that is worth interrupting their engagement with texts?

With this book, *Conferring with Readers: Supporting Each Student's Growth and Independence,* Gravity and Jen make suggestions for what we can teach that can make a difference in a reader's life. They explain ways we can learn more about what and how a reader reads. Jen and Gravity discuss the strategies and processes many strong readers use. They present ways to select one thing a reader needs next on the road to becoming an even better reader. And finally, they offer methods to teach that information (or process or idea) to the reader.

Jen and Gravity draw upon their years of experience as teachers and with teachers in the Teachers College Reading and Writing Project community. As members of that community, they have often wrestled with these questions of how to work with individual readers, of how to teach children to get better at doing something when you can't even see them doing it. In this book, they have put forth some of the best practices we have invented over the past decade to help teachers understand ways children read and ways to help them read better.

In this book, Jen and Gravity offer us scaffolds to help us hold individual reading conferences with our students, one-on-one conversations that can empower our readers to strengthen their understandings and responses to texts. That in itself makes this book a rare and valuable resource for every teacher. Perhaps the greatest gift this book can offer, however, is that with the reading of it, we teachers may find in our own hearts and minds the courage to interrupt what is good to strive for what is great.

—Lucy Calkins

What It Means to Be a Reader

"Leslie was huddled next to one of the cracks below the roof trying to get enough light to read."

— BRIDGE TO TERABITHIA, BY KATHERINE PATERSON

Stop for a minute and let your mind drift back to the times in your life when reading mattered, the times when you were so totally engrossed in a book that it was more important than the phone ringing, the hungry grumbles in your stomach, or your favorite TV show starting. Remember a time when you were so lost in a book, you stayed up all night long to finish it. Remember a time you cheered out loud for a character. Remember a time you and your son fell asleep in bed while you were reading to him; you awoke several hours later with the book squished in between the two of you.

I have clear pictures from my own reading life, from the lives of my friends and colleagues, and from my students of what it looks like, feels like, and sounds like to be a reader. While there is no clear one way to live as a reader, my thinking does tend to fall into three main categories.

I believe:

- Reading is the act of constructing meaning;
- Reading is a process; and
- Reading is deeply personal and, therefore, varies from reader to reader.

Reading Is the Act of Constructing Meaning

While I believe that a strong knowledge of phonics and phonemic awareness is important for all readers, I see a huge difference between calling out words and reading. I agree with Cambourne's (1988) definition—"reading is meaning." Reading is the act of constructing meaning from a text in an ongoing dialogue between the reader and the text, and between the reader and other readers. When a person reads, she constructs meaning from a text based on her own experiences, knowledge, and interest. In a way, then, the "reader writes the story"(Harvey & Goudvis 2000). Understanding comes from the dialogue that a reader has with the text in the process of constructing meaning. Children, even at the youngest ages, are constructing meaning from texts when they look closely at the pictures and tell the story or read the simple words on the page and react to what they say with giggles. Readers don't have to be able to read the character's name to talk about the character's motivations, traits, and obstacles.

I'll never forget when I was ten years old, cuddled up in my Mickey Mouse blanket on my back porch reading *Bridge to Terabithia.* I imagined what it would be like to swing across the gully on an old rope into a magical land. I would occasionally glance up from the pages long enough to close my eyes and pretend that I was the queen. As my eyes glued back to the pages and I read further, I found myself weeping: I wasn't just tearing up, but full-on weeping. My mom rushed into the room and asked me what was wrong, but all I could say was, "She can't be dead." I was angry at Katherine Paterson and seriously thought about writing her a letter to tell her how unfair it was to kill off my friend . . . after all, Leslie did feel like my friend. I don't just read about characters, but form judgments, make connections, and develop feelings for them. Some of my first loves were the characters in books. I learned what it means to have a best friend from *Bridge to Terabithia* and what it means to lose one.

Later, in my early teen years, I, along with many other students in my school, discovered the *Sweet Valley High* series. While I can look back and see these books were not the most challenging books I read, they did help me see the social aspects of reading. In school, my friends and I were required to read from anthologies of stories that we had little interest in, but at home we read as many *Sweet Valley High* books as we could convince our parents to buy. I would read book one and then trade with Janine for book two. I read book after book and then bunny-eared my favorite pages or wrote hearts and smiles in the margins so I could later share parts with Janine, Cristin, and Erin. The *Sweet Valley High* characters were blond, popular twins who dated handsome and popular boys. Our sixth-grade selves would talk for hours about what it must be like to drive convertibles and go on dates. As I read about the latest drama in the twins' lives, I would have conversations in my head with them: "Why would you do that? How could you take him back?" As I read, I was constantly speaking to the characters or preparing to have conversations with fellow readers. The best books I've read made me run to the phone or interrupt my friend next to me. I couldn't wait to talk about them. In many ways, the conversations about the *Sweet Valley* twins prompted my first conversations about puberty, love, and the fears and excitement associated with growing up.

Reading Is a Process

While reading, people have strategies for understanding their books that allow them to construct meaning and learn from the texts while also learning more about themselves. Readers have strategies for figuring out what the words say on the page and what they mean. They have strategies for dealing with difficult words, phrases, and confusing parts. They have strategies for remembering key characters, events, and facts, and for accumulating the key information when needed. They have strategies for thinking about the text and forming judgments and opinions as they read. Readers employ many strategies—some that are automatic and some they need to think about—in order to construct the meaning of the text.

All athletes have strategies. As a former collegiate soccer player, I sat with my teammates and studied videotapes of our games and of our opponents. We listened as our coach taught us different plays. Each play became a strategy we could employ when needed. For example, if our team was playing against a team with a short goalie, we would choose a strategy of shooting the ball high in the air (presumably over the goalie's head). But, if we encountered a tall goalie, we had to be able to adjust our strategy and choose another play. Good readers do the same. They have a series of plays stored away in their memories. As soccer players, we accumulated hundreds of plays to choose from during the course of a game, just as readers have accumulated hundreds of strategies to choose from during the course of reading a text. The best readers can try a strategy and, if it does not help, try another one and another one until they understand. My soccer coach called this tenacity—the ability and desire to keep trying and adapting until we figured out what would work. Readers, then, must be tenacious and strive to keep trying strategies until they find the ones that work for them.

Tatianna is one of these readers. She loved to read adventure books. Although she lived a fairly nonadventurous third-grade life, she enjoyed reading books about characters who took risks. Tatianna read one of the *Magic Treehouse* books and decided it was one of her new favorites. Once she learned there were many books in this series and that she could continue reading about Annie (her favorite character), she was thrilled. But Tatianna would not return a *Magic Treehouse* book to the classroom library once she read it. She hoarded the books in her own personal bag of books and often reread sections of them. I realized that Tatianna had written Post-it notes with her thoughts and placed them all over the books. She did not want to return the books because she did not want to forget her thinking. After I explained to Tatianna that other students in the class wanted to read those books, she got an idea. Tatianna decided to start a section in her reading notebook that was dedicated to *Magic Treehouse* books. She wrote the title of each book on a new page of the notebook and placed her important Post-it thoughts on the pages. This new strategy allowed her to reread her notes after returning the books, thus allowing others to read the books as well.

Reading Is Deeply Personal and, Therefore, Varies from Reader to Reader

Although all readers are constructing meaning and employing strategies as they read, the decisions they make and the opinions they form vary from reader to reader. A few months ago I sat in a room full of my colleagues where we discussed our favorite and least favorite books. I heard one staff developer explain why she hated the book *Life of Pi*. In the middle of her explanation of why she disliked the book, another colleague literally gasped: She could not understand how someone could hate that book. She passionately described why *Life of Pi* was one of the most important books she had read. During the two drastically different explanations, both readers gave personal reasons why they did or did not connect to the book. While it was evident that both readers constructed meaning of the text and followed a process of using strategies, they both ultimately had deeply personal experiences with the book—one positive and one negative.

There are always facts in books. Winnie the Pooh is a bear, and he has a friend named Piglet. Most readers would not dispute these statements. But how I think and react to the facts as a reader is quite different. What I think about Pooh and Piglet's relationship, if I agree with the characters' decisions, and how I bring my own knowledge of friendship to bear on my opinions of them is quite different. There is no correct reaction to characters and no one interpretation of Pooh and Piglet's relationship. Readers are unique individuals and, therefore, their interpretations and opinions of a text will be unique and varied.

Recently I finished a reading conference with a timid first grader and then stepped back and observed her from afar with her classroom teacher. We watched as she lingered on each page of her *Biscuit* book. She covered the words at the bottom of the page and studied the picture. When Biscuit the dog tugged on his owner's shirt, she smiled and let out a little chuckle. Then she moved her hands, uncovering the few simple words on the page, and read each one in a little doggy voice.

When I began reading *Seabiscuit,* the true story of a racehorse and the men involved in his racing career (the owner, trainer, and jockey), I didn't care much about horse racing and had never paid much attention to it. I had never even watched the Kentucky Derby on TV. But, as I turned page after page of the book, I found myself connecting to the story in surprising ways. As a former sprinter in high school and college, I recalled the feelings on race day: the anxiety as I put on my racing shoes, the adrenaline as I approached the starting line, and the cockiness of believing I would outrun the others. As I read about Seabiscuit and his jockey on race day, I imagined how they must have felt: anxious, full of adrenaline, and a little cocky. When Seabiscuit won, I felt pride, as if I somehow had something to do with the success. When he lost, I felt a terrible disappointment that only someone who has trained hard and lost can truly feel. In many ways I was on the emotional seesaw along with Seabiscuit, his jockey, and his fans. After reading *Seabiscuit,* I felt like I had raced in the Kentucky Derby and that I had been the fastest and best, even if it was for a short time. While I never was the best sprinter, I could feel the sheer joy of what it would have been like to be the best. Another reader who already knew a lot about Seabiscuit and followed his career or a reader who dislikes competition would likely have a very different reaction to this book.

✳✳✳

As you read these pages, I hope you remembered the times reading really mattered to you. I hope you didn't just visualize the cover of a book, but also the relationships you built, the emotions you felt, and the conversations you had. It's important to hold onto these memories as you reflect on the kind of reading you want in your classroom.

It can be daunting to create a classroom where all readers build relationships with characters, encounter new experiences and emotions, and have conversations with books and other readers, but I know it is possible. Taking five minutes at least once a week to sit with every young reader offers you the opportunity to accomplish the lofty goals of fostering lifelong readers. It offers you the opportunity to make instructional decisions that match the individual reader and to choose methods that grow and change along with the student. Reading conferring is a time you can open up your reading life to children and invite them to take a peek. You are not only teaching students strategies, but also showing them the power of reading.

My hope is that as you read this book and prepare for reading conferences in your own classroom, you will make more time to read yourself. I hope you dust off that book on your bed stand or drive to the nearest bookstore. After all, you are the mentor reader in your classroom, and your reading life will inspire your students to do the same: to go to the library or give that dusty book a second chance.

What It Means to Teach Reading

"Children should learn that reading is pleasure, not just something that teachers make you do in school."

— BEVERLY CLEARY

A recent National Endowment for the Arts study found that reading, to more than half of all Americans, isn't something they do outside of school. The survey found that fewer than half of Americans read literature, and the decline in reading rates for people ages eighteen to twenty-four fell fifty-five percent from the last survey, done only twenty years earlier. Americans *can* read—we have a literacy rate of about ninety-nine percent—it's just that Americans *don't like* to read.

This is a crisis.

As a teacher, I need to do my best to create lifelong engaged readers who value time spent reading alone, and time spent sharing their reading with others. To do this, I believe I need to create opportunities for them to feel successful with books right away, and to act as a model reader, a *mentor,* along their journey.

Through my years in the classroom and as a staff developer with the Teachers College Reading and Writing Project (TCRWP), working closely alongside Lucy Calkins, Kathleen Tolan, and a staff of literacy leaders, I have learned a great deal about engaging students in reading and teaching them to read well. I believe:

- Reading instruction should match the individual reader;
- Reading instruction should teach toward independence;
- Reading instruction should explicitly teach strategies to access skills;

- Reading instruction should value time for reading, volume of reading, and variety of reading experiences; and
- Reading instruction should follow predictable structures and routines.

I fully admit that none of these beliefs is original. In writing this book, I stand on the shoulders of countless researchers, staff developers, and teachers, both published and unpublished. In each of the sections that follow, I review what some of these people have to say about reading and the teaching of reading in the context of my tenets.

Reading Instruction Should Match the Individual Reader

Reading instruction that values the individual is instruction that allows students to choose their own books that are of interest and at an appropriate reading level. Individualized instruction is deeply rooted in assessment, with reading skills and strategies that are taught based on what the student needs most. While I also believe time needs to be set aside each day for whole-class teaching in read-alouds and minilessons, there also needs to be ample time for individualized instruction.

I was not taught to read as an individual. If you're like me, you might have spent reading time in elementary school in some kind of a reading group. At my elementary school, we had the red rockets, the bluebirds, and the airplanes. My teachers grouped us according to our state test scores, and we all read the same excerpts of books from an anthology. Because there were only a few groups in the whole class, even within our group we had a variety of reading levels. One or two kids always dominated the group, while a couple of others would sit back quietly struggling to understand the story.

Then, later in elementary school and in middle school and high school, I moved from being part of a reading group to studying one novel at a time together with my class. I read *The Adventures of Tom Sawyer*, *To Kill a Mockingbird*, and *Ulysses*. I was assigned vocabulary words that I had to locate in the currently assigned book, find definitions for in a dictionary, and put into sentences in my reading notebook. I read an assigned number of pages each night and answered questions about the book on tests. I must admit that I was a frequent buyer of CliffsNotes.

The first part of individualizing is helping students to choose their own books that are at an appropriate level and are of interest. There is widespread agreement among many researchers that students deserve opportunities to read books that they can read with fluency and comprehension (Allington 2001; Calkins 2001; Collins 2005; Fountas and Pinnell 2006). Students deserve to choose books that they can read with fluency, accuracy, and comprehension, and in which they are interested. Reading workshop teachers often label their classroom library books according to reading level to help students choose just-right books. There are different ways to level books, such as Reading Recovery Levels, Guided Reading Levels, and the Teachers College Reading and Writing Project's Groups (Peterson 2001; Fountas and Pinnell 1996; Calkins 2002).

There is more to individualizing book choice than just the reading level of the text. Many teachers have found that students can pick up a few different books at the same level and read some with more fluency, accuracy, and comprehension than others. A student's interest and background knowledge plays heavily into his ability to read a text, so students therefore should be taught to choose just-right books not only on the basis of reading level but also on interest level. Readers will discover the authors they love and choose other books by the same author. They will take advice from other readers about books they just have to pick up and read. They will discover some topics of interest that they love to learn about and read to become more knowledgeable in that topic.

In addition to choosing just-right books, individualizing in a reading workshop also refers to the type of instruction students should receive. Richard Allington, author of *What Matters Most for Struggling Readers* (2001), has what he terms a one hundred/one hundred goal: He wishes that all schools had a goal of educating one hundred percent of the students in reading instruction that is appropriate to their needs and development one hundred percent of the time. A reading workshop is the perfect place to meet this goal.

Reading conferences are often one-on-one work with a student in which instruction is individualized to support her strengths and help to push her to the edge of what she's just beginning to be able to do. In the beginning of the year, my goal is to get to know each reader well. I have conferences with each reader to determine his reading level and the types of books that fit his or her interests. Then, through a series of conferences across the entire year about books the reader has chosen, I get to know each student's reading life even better. Part of this is asking questions that dig deep at a reader's process to uncover the invisible work she is doing as a reader, to develop an individualized plan for her, and to carefully choose teaching methods that match his or her learning style. Regardless of the situation in which the instruction takes place, it is vital that each reader is seen and treated as an individual. Even when working inside of whole-class studies where I teach one minilesson to the entire class, I still leave substantial time to differentiate my teaching in individualized reading conferences.

Reading Instruction Should Teach Toward Independence

Many teachers, when asked their goals for their students as readers, will answer that they want their students to become lifelong lovers of reading. "I hope that my students will carry books with them everywhere and pull them out on the subway train," they say. They hope that on vacation at the beach their students could be caught reading their favorite series book under the shade of an umbrella. They hope that their students will have the necessary skills to follow a recipe, read the daily newspaper, or maybe even join a book club discussion group. In order for students to be lifelong lovers of reading, we need to put ourselves out of business as teachers. Reading workshops, and specifically conferences, are our opportunities as teachers to act as mentors to readers toward that goal.

One of the aspects of becoming an independent reader is to know how to choose books that fit you. But there is more to it than that. To be truly independent, students need to know how to get themselves out of trouble when they face difficulty in a text. In order for students to be successful independent readers, they use strategies for reading automatically and metacognatively in order to comprehend texts. Students learn to use everything they know in concert to make meaning of texts.

In *When Kids Can't Read, What Teachers Can Do* (2003), Kylene Beers articulates the difference between independent and dependent readers. She says that what makes a reader independent depends on what happens when he encounters difficulty. An independent reader will "figure out what's confusing him, set goals for getting through the reading, use many strategies for getting through the text, and know how to make the mostly invisible process of reading visible." On the other hand, dependent readers will "stop, appeal to the teacher, read through, and keep the invisible process of reading mostly invisible" (Beers 2003, 16).

In order to foster independence, I set up conditions in my classroom to make it possible. Brian Cambourne identified conditions whereby students acquire language, readers learn to read, and writers learn to write. Two of these conditions, "expectation" and "responsibility," relate directly to the goal of independence. I need to be clear with my expectation that every student *will* learn to read. I need to communicate this by setting aside a lot of time for reading each day and encouraging students to be problem-solvers by themselves when they encounter difficulty. I must also hold students accountable for the specific strategies I teach in minilessons and in conferences. Students are responsible for what they've been taught and are supported less and less as they apply strategies they've learned to independent reading.

Having high expectations, though, does not mean that I can demand perfection from students. Another of Cambourne's conditions is "approximation." I expect that students will make their best attempt at applying new learning to their reading each day, and my job is to provide support and mentorship as they read with greater independence.

In reading conferences my goal is to make sure that each reader is not only using strategies, but also using them independently and with confidence. In reading conferences, I ask questions and observe readers closely to find out what they are securely doing and what they are approximating. I choose compliments and teaching points to support students as they develop reading behaviors, processes, and strategies that build toward independence. It is important that each conference isn't teaching something brand new; instead many conferences follow up and build on what readers learned in the past.

Reading Instruction Should Explicitly Teach Strategies to Access Skills

Proficient readers carry a set of reading skills and strategies with them when they approach any text. In order to make meaning of a text, readers make use of strategies and decide when a given strategy is appropriate. Ellin Oliver Keene and Susan Zimmermann, in their book *Mosaic of Thought* (1997), distilled the process of reading down to seven reading strategies that proficient readers use to construct meaning from texts. They found that readers must activate prior knowledge; determine the most important ideas and themes in a text; create visual and sensory images before, during, and after reading; draw inferences from the text; retell and synthesize what they've read; ask questions of the text and themselves as they read; and use fix-up strategies when comprehension breaks down.

At the TCRWP we call Keene and Zimmermann's list of strategies reading *skills*. Skills are applicable to all reading texts and experiences. For example, the skill of determining importance can be used in a newspaper article or a novel. We call the different ways *how* a reader performs a skill a reading strategy. A strategy is one way a reader can perform a skill. There are many different strategies for each reading skill, and they are dependent on the kind of texts a person is reading, and the reader's own set of prior experiences and reading processes.

Kathleen Tolan, deputy director of the TCRWP, is a master at explaining reading strategies. She taught us that it is not enough to tell a reader to use a skill such as visualization. We need to teach the reader a strategy for how to visualize. We may tell the student to visualize *by* paying attention to the way that the author has described the setting or to visualize a character's face *by* matching the facial expressions to the emotions the character is feeling in the scene. A strategy explicitly states the steps for how to use the skill.

My role as a teacher of reading is to do more than just name strategies for students. I also model proficient reading by demonstrating strategies and help students by coaching them through difficulty and gradually releasing scaffolding as appropriate (Cambourne 1988; Beers 2003). Linda Fielding and David Pearson's (1994) research shows that an important part of reading instruction involves the gradual release of responsibility along a gradient. This begins with modeling and moves to guided practice where the teacher and student do the work together. Finally, independent practice is expected as the reader applies what was learned to other real reading situations.

The reading conference is a time for me to explicitly teach students reading strategies. I demonstrate how to use a strategy, coach the reader through difficulty, and release supports as appropriate. In a reading conference, I have a skill in mind and teach an appropriate strategy for how to perform the skill. Often,

I focus on one skill over time by varying my teaching methods inside of the conference or by teaching different strategies for the same skill.

Reading Instruction Should Value Time for Reading, Volume of Reading, and Variety of Reading Experiences

It's the old adage, "practice makes perfect." It seems to make perfect common sense—the more time we give someone to do something, the better she gets at it. Cambourne calls it the condition of "employment"—that we give students plenty of opportunity to practice what we taught. This is not just a saying or a theory; research confirms that it holds true for reading as well. Allington (2001) found that there is a direct correlation between the amount of time spent reading and reading performance.

Allington (2001) advises that students should spend ninety minutes each day in school reading—not hearing about reading, not responding to reading, not talking about reading, but actually *reading*. Unfortunately, though, it is often the case that students who are already reading below grade-level benchmarks get pulled out of class for more word attack instruction, phonics instruction, or are involved in more reading groups where a lot of the time is spent with the teacher introducing the book. The consequence here is that students spend less time actually reading. Readers in upper elementary grades have another hurdle to overcome as well. During content areas like science and social studies, whole-class materials such as textbooks are often written at a reading level considered to be at or above grade level. Because some readers can't actually read these too-hard texts they are holding, the time spent with them is not really reading.

In Calkins' reading workshop model, many hours every week are devoted to students reading books at their just-right reading level. All readers spend a significant amount of time with their eyes on print, attempting to transfer what they've been taught to their own chosen material while being coached through difficulty. Students spend a good deal of time reading books that are aligned to the current content of the whole-class study and may also spend time reading other genres. Sometimes students will be purposefully rereading; other times they'll be reading a new text or continuing a text they started the day before. In either case, what they are reading are real books, not basal readers or Dick and Jane–type books that are artificially crafted for reading instruction. Ideally, each day's reading workshop lasts one full hour, with only ten minutes carved away for a minilesson, and five minutes or so for the share. (I do realize, however, that in some schools a reading workshop may be more like forty-five minutes.) The remaining forty-five minutes is spent on independent reading and conferring, with some time set aside for partnerships or book clubs.

Deciding to confer, then, is a commitment to the kind of classroom where reading volume matters. In a reading workshop, I move around the room, conferring with individuals, pairs, or small groups and then leave them to practice after five to ten minutes of direct instruction or guided practice. I will often incorporate reading book logs and having discussions about volume as part of my regular conferring practice to reinforce the importance of reading a lot.

Reading Instruction Should Follow Predictable Structures and Routines

We at the TCRWP have developed predictable structures and routines that foster effective reading instruction, outlined in Calkins' *The Art of Teaching Reading* (2001). I strongly recommend this model of reading workshop, although I recognize that some may choose other structures and routines. What I believe is most important is that reading instruction fosters independence—that students explicitly are taught strategies and given a lot of time for independent practice.

Structure is essential in reading conferences. The structure of a conference helps keep me on task, and allows the student to be freed up to listen to the content because he can predict the way the conference goes every time. Beyond that, I want to make sure that there are structures in place in the entire workshop, and routines that allow for conferring to happen. These structures have helped my conferences to be efficient and effective. In our work as staff developers, we usually begin by helping teachers use "an architecture" for different structures like individual and small-group conferring. I tend to use what we call the "research, decide, teach" conference. First, I research the reader's process and strategies. Then I decide what compliment to give the reader, what strategy to teach the reader, and what method of instruction I will use. Finally, I teach the reader a strategy to help her toward using it with independence.

My goal is for every student to see reading the way Beverly Cleary does: as pleasure. Designing reading instruction around the previous five tenets can foster lifelong readers who continue reading even when it is not required. In the fast-paced, standards-driven school climate in which I teach, reading conferences provide a way to meet individual students' needs in manageable and meaningful ways.

3

Getting Ready: Management and Structures

"We have so much time and so little to do. Strike that, reverse it."
— CHARLIE AND THE CHOCOLATE FACTORY, BY ROALD DAHL

Picture it: a class of thirty-two students. All readers are holding books that they have chosen. A pack of Post-it notes and a reading notebook is nearby each student and many of them have pens in their hands as they read. They're each snuggled into spots around the classroom, engrossed in their books. Across the room a student giggles at a funny part in her book, while another reader has his mouth wide open in surprise. Martin, the classroom teacher, is moving around the room, following up with a few readers he met with earlier in the workshop. He taps one student's book, reminding her to read the section headings before reading the rest of the page. He reads over a note a boy wrote on a Post-it and gives a nod, a thumbs-up, and a smile. He has a binder in his hands filled with conferring notes and the class read-aloud tucked under his arm to pull out at a moment's notice. Martin wanders to the back corner of the room where there's a partnership of readers sitting back-to-back reading the same chapter, writing Post-it notes to prepare for their conversations. "Hey, readers, can I interrupt your reading for a minute?" he begins.

To create this kind of community—where there is a commitment to independence, an expectation of academic rigor, and a high level of productivity—there are predictable routines and structures that can be taught. While any teacher who has students reading self-chosen books at an appropriate reading level can try out the reading conferences described in this book, I recommend a reading workshop, as described by Lucy Calkins in *The Art of Teaching Reading* (2001) and by Kathy Collins in *Growing Readers* (2004). A reading workshop is a set of structures used daily. These structures often are used as a method to teach a yearly curriculum for reading, frequently centering on month-long whole-class studies, which are described in Chapter 6.

The Reading Workshop

I have fond memories of my high school art teacher, Ken Vieth. He always began class by gathering us around him to demonstrate the work of the day. "By beginning with this grid on the face you have drawn," he would say, "you can make sure that you are placing the features in correct proportions on your portraits." After a brief class meeting, he'd send us off to work on our own portraits. During this time, he'd move around the room reacting to our work as "successful!" and giving us tips and hints to push us. For the student next to me, it might be to consider the re-placement of the hairline by using other features on the face as a guide. But for me, it might have been to bring more reality to the portrait by paying more attention to the shading on the cheekbones. Class ended with Mr. Vieth sharing some examples of student work and using those examples to help us each with our own work. Sometimes we worked collaboratively with partners, and sometimes we worked on our own pieces, but I always worked near others who would help me, support me, and critique me.

In art, I moved through units of study—clay, portrait art, sculpture, watercolors, collage. We produced lots and lots of work. My artwork improved dramatically across each year that I was in Mr. Vieth's class because I had a lot of encouragement, practice, and teaching that was tailored to my needs. And today, if I sit down to paint a landscape or take a photograph, I definitely have Mr. Vieth's voice in the back of my head, although I know I'm on my own. This type of teaching, and the conditions that he set up in his classroom, are exactly the conditions that Brian Cambourne (1988) writes about, and are exactly the conditions I try to create in a reading workshop.

Thousands of teachers from New York City to Shanghai have become familiar with a workshop approach to teaching writing, and many of them have begun teaching reading in a similar structure. They believe, as I do, that students learn best by actually doing, with support and instruction along the way. When writing workshop was first begun, it was actually called the "conference approach" to teaching writing because of the importance placed on independence with individualized support from the teacher. This applies, too, to reading workshop.

Reading workshop lasts forty-five to sixty minutes every day, and within that time there is a predictable structure. The structures of the workshop model are described very briefly in the following sections because of the importance of contextualizing conferring.

In a reading workshop, the class begins workshop time by gathering together for a brief lesson, called a "minilesson," much in the same way that Mr. Vieth gathered his art students to learn about ensuring symmetry in portrait drawing. Here, the teacher directly teaches the students for about seven minutes by demonstrating a strategy and allowing them to have a quick try. The topics for these minilessons come from month-long whole-class studies, and from the teacher's assessments of what most of his class needs. Many find it helpful to refer to Lucy Calkins' *Units of Study in Primary Writing* (2003) and *Units of Study for Teaching Writing* (2006) book sets. In these books, she clearly lays out a helpful architecture for minilessons.

After this brief gathering, students go off to their independent reading spots, where they practice the strategy from the minilesson in combination with other strategies they've learned while they read books that they've chosen themselves. On some days readers meet with partnerships or with clubs who are reading the same book to discuss questions that have come up as they've read; they analyze and interpret, retell, or troubleshoot where comprehension broke down. Students may also spend a small portion of the workshop writing in response to their reading—either jotting quick notes to themselves on Post-its that stay in their books, freewriting in their reading notebooks to deepen comprehension, or taking notes that may help to improve their upcoming conversations with their partner or club.

It is during the independent time that I make my way around the classroom to confer with individuals, partners, and clubs. In between conferences I will walk the room to refocus students, give words of encouragement to others, and to check in on readers with whom I've conferred to hold them accountable for what I taught. During this time I carry around my notes so I can jot down assessment information from my conferences and observations of my research when watching the room. Developing a note-taking system is described in more detail in Chapter 12. I choose not to use this time for my own independent reading; while students are reading I am busy individualizing instruction for everyone in the room.

The final five or so minutes of the workshop are spent in a whole-class teaching share in which I gather the readers back together and use student work and experiences from the day to illustrate a teaching point. This teaching point may follow up on the minilesson, address a common challenge for the class that arose that day, or set up for the work of tomorrow. Sometimes I'll summarize some of what I observed or talked about with readers and I'll ask a few students to share examples. Other times, I'll ask a partnership or club to rewind a conversation they had so that we can all observe and learn from the work they did. On occasion, I'll simply celebrate an aspect of their work. The share allows students to mentor each other and to be seen as reading experts with important reading strategies to teach.

The Classroom Library

Over the past three years, New York City public schools have been committed to teaching reading in a reading workshop. Many of these schools have found that one of the biggest challenges to a reading workshop is resources. Unlike a writing workshop—where you can function with a notebook, some paper, and a pencil—having a strong reading workshop requires books. A *lot* of books. These books should be organized into a classroom library so that students can easily find books that match them as readers. This will allow them to spend less time *looking for* books and more time *reading* books.

To determine the number of books and the types of books I need, I look at my yearly curriculum and the reading levels of the students in my class. During years when I taught kindergarten through second grade, or when I taught grades three through five but with high numbers of struggling readers, I needed more books than when I taught a class of fifth graders reading at grade level. This requirement is simply because books at lower levels are very short and students can read them quickly. I have a classroom library with enough books for each student in my class to have a week's worth of books at a time—for students reading short beginning chapter books like *Frog and Toad*, that's about ten books; for students reading longer chapter books like *Shiloh*, that's more like two books. (For more information on reading volume correlated to levels, see Richard Allington's *What Really Matters for Struggling Readers* [2001]). Next, I look at my yearly curriculum to decide when I'll have my students reading in partnerships. When they meet in partnerships, I need two copies of each title because they will read and discuss the same book. And during book-club time, I need four to five copies of each title for the same reason.

It's also important that my classroom library reflects a wide range of genres and interests that my students might have. I never shy away from fairy tales, comic books, graphic novels, or magazines. It's true that the readers in my class probably spend a good amount of time each day reading material that is supported by my whole-class study, but it is also important that they are in the practice of reading many kinds of material, as real readers do. I also find that it sometimes helps to engage some of my more reluctant readers if they have more of a choice in what they can borrow and read.

Once I have my books, I plan on an organizational system that helps readers to choose their books quickly and effectively. I want to help students choose "just-right" books that are at their reading level and are of interest to them. For that reason, I try to level as many of my books as possible.

While there are several different book leveling systems, I decide on one system—either DRA levels, Reading Recovery levels, or Fountas and Pinnell Guided Reading levels—and then I stick to it. Next, I use a combination of one of many free websites online where I can type in the title or author of the book and get the level. If I choose to level my library according to Fountas and Pinnell's levels, then I will rely heavily on their guide (2005).

Once I decide on a system for leveling books, and look up the titles in a reputable source, I next mark the books so students will be able to easily choose them. Some teachers decide to write the level right on the front cover or inside the front cover in permanent marker. Other teachers develop a color-coding system and place colored dots on the cover. Whatever you decide, keep in mind that readers most often will be choosing "just-right" books from the library, and a library that's clearly marked will help to facilitate choosing.

Next I organize my books into bins or baskets. I use some low bookshelves (no higher than my students' shoulder-height) or sideways milk crates to hold baskets that are labeled. Some baskets may be labeled simply with the reading level, whereas others may be labeled with a favorite author, a series, or a genre. Many teachers choose to have the baskets labeled with pictures if their class is made up of many English language learners or students who cannot conventionally read labels. Shana Frazin, a colleague at the Reading and Writing Project, often encourages teachers to think of creative names for baskets like "Hey! I never knew that!" for a basket containing nonfiction books. I also like to include some of my own students' writing in a basket labeled "authors from our classroom."

I never want my readers to visit the classroom library during independent reading time. Every minute is precious, so book-shopping time, as we call it, happens at another time of the day. I tell students how many books they should take for a week's worth of home and school reading. As I mentioned earlier, this number depends on their reading level, with students reading at lower levels taking more books (because they are shorter and meant to be read more quickly) and students reading at higher levels taking fewer books.

Figure 3-1. Ms. Friedman's second grade classroom library at P.S. 63.

When we are in a whole-class study revolving around partnerships or clubs, the students visit the classroom library with their partners or clubs and choose the books they'll be reading together as well as the books they'll read independently. They keep their week's worth of books in a baggie or magazine bin that they easily can access in the classroom. If I want to avoid students telling me that they are done, I have to make sure they have enough books for the week.

Making Student Thinking Visible—Written Structures

Reading and thinking about reading are invisible, but I can create some structures that help me to see what's going on in my students' heads. These structures can be used as part of my research during a conference, and they can be collected and studied periodically. What I notice from my students' writing about their reading can help me to get ready for conferences or small-group work, and helps me to hold my students accountable for past teaching.

Book Logs

Reading rate and reading volume matter. Allington (2001) argues that one of the biggest determinants of later success in reading is the amount of time and the number of words that you read each day as a young reader. For this reason, it makes sense to have some systematic way to help students to keep track of what they're reading. I recommend that your book log has the following categories, though you may adapt it depending on the grade level of the students you teach:

- Date
- Title
- Author
- Level
- Location (home or school?)
- Number of minutes spent reading
- Number of pages read

Date	Title	Author	Level	H or S?	# Min.?	# Pgs.?

Volume, stamina, and reading rate matter tremendously, but they should never take the place of comprehension. I do not want students speeding through books at the expense of understanding what they read. Instead, I want readers moving along through their books at a consistent rate. In Chapter 10, I go into more detail on how to take the information from these logs and use them to inform your instruction.

Post-It Notes

As adults, many of us read with pens in our hands. When reading for graduate classes, we underline and jot in the margins to summarize or react to what's been written. When I get ready for a book-club meeting, I put stars in the margin, write down questions for discussion, and record brief retellings so that I can reference parts easily during discussion. Because most of the books that readers are holding at school are teacher- or school- owned, the next best thing to jotting in the margins is jotting on a Post-it note. Students can write questions, comments, reactions, and retellings on Post-its and leave them in their books until they meet with the teacher, a partner, or a book club. Having Post-its with their thinking right next to the spot in the text that led them to those thoughts helps readers to reference text easily, and allows me as a teacher to see the origin of their thinking. I often begin conferences by asking students to show me what they've been jotting about their reading and to talk to me about some of their ideas. When a student is ready to return a book to the classroom library, she can peel the Post-it notes from her book and keep them in a notebook or folder for safekeeping.

The Reading Notebook

Many authors have recognized the importance of students writing about their reading as a way to hold onto and grow their thinking (Angelillo 2003; Calkins 2001). The writing is a vehicle for clarifying their thoughts about what they read, for preparing for conversations with other readers, and for holding themselves accountable to what they've been taught.

The reading notebook serves as a place to hold students' thinking about their reading across time. Some teachers might direct students to use a reading notebook in place of Post-it notes to jot their thoughts as they read, with the benefit to this approach being that, for younger readers, it's easier to manage the materials and often less expensive than buying many pads of Post-it notes (Figure 3-2). Many students use reading notebooks as places to write longer entries that flesh out ideas about an author's meaning, theories about a character, or some connections that they're making about the books (Figure 3-3). These longer entries may be the starting off point for essays about the books they're reading, or simply a place to clarify their thinking or to play around with

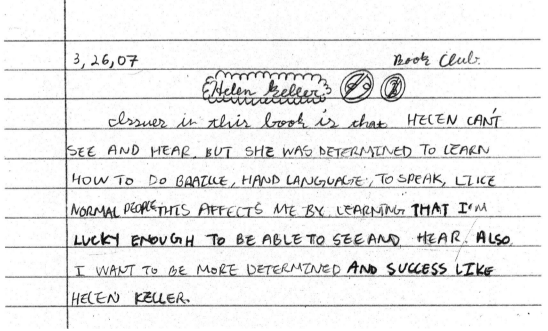

Figure 3-2. One fifth grader's notebook entry to prepare for her biography book club meeting.

Oliver Button is a sissy 2-16-07

Melissa 2-16-07 ①

I think oliver is individu,
because everyone thinks;
boys have to do
tough things but
he likes doing
girl things e.g. oliver
was playing dress-up
and his dad said he
had to play a sport.

oliver button is
indivisual because all the
boys are doing sports and
rough things but Oliver
Button is doing girl things
like ; Dress-up and playing
with dolls. And everyone
thinks boys have to do
rough things but Oliver
just likes to do girl
things. and that doesn't
mean he is a sissy. He is
just being his self, being
who he is, being individual
and having fun the way he
likes to have fun.

Figure 3-3. A page from Melissa's notebook. She's taken an important Post-it from her independent reading book and written an extended response.

ideas in preparation for meeting with a partnership or club. If they use Post-its, I have students remove the important ones from their books and attach them to pages in their notebooks with headings that include the date, author, and title of the books so their thinking isn't lost. The reading notebook may also be a place where students set goals for themselves as readers, or reflect upon their own reading identity. I must be careful in reading workshop to not allow the notebook to completely overtake independent reading time. The notebook is a tool for *very brief* writing about reading—the thrust of the time in a workshop should still be spent with students reading or talking about their books. Every day, I strive to have my students sustain reading for at least a half hour, and most days it is more like forty-five minutes.

Managing a Class of Independent Readers

Teach Students Their Roles When They're Independently Reading

If I want readers to manage themselves and carry on independently in a workshop, it's helpful to make sure that I've taught them what I'm expecting. I learned from Colleen Cruz, a colleague at the TCRWP, that it's helpful to anticipate potential problems that would stand in the way of independence and plan how I can handle these problems proactively. If I am clear on what my expectations are and I share them with the readers, then a lot of problems will be nipped in the bud. It's also helpful, she taught me, to consider what would happen if my best-laid plans were to fail. I need a plan for what my reaction will be so that I don't waste precious reading and conferring time putting out fires.

In my own classroom, I could anticipate the following potential problems:

- Students will tell me, "I'm finished reading all my books."
- Students will tell me someone's bothering them and they can't concentrate.
- Students will ask to use the bathroom or to get a drink of water.
- Students will ask me for supplies like Post-it notes and pencils.

- Students will run out of steam and start to become bored or distracted.
- Students will want to share their thinking with a friend nearby and will begin talking.

I plan to be proactive in my classroom. I first teach students in a minilesson at the beginning of the year (and again whenever it's needed) that their role in a reading workshop is to read independently. During this time they are allowed to read only the books they have chosen from the library, to reread when they feel finished, and to jot down their thinking about their books. In many classrooms, they are not allowed to enter into conversations with others about their books until partnership and club time.

In kindergarten and first-grade classrooms, students are reading independently, but often out loud to themselves, and are given a separate time to read aloud to one another. Because students' reading stamina is often low because they read for smaller amounts of time before they share, teachers find it helpful to alternate between independent reading and partner reading a few times during the reading time so that students are focused on reading the entire time, but in different genres and for different purposes.

I teach students the routine in my classroom for using the bathroom and getting a drink of water—I personally allow my readers to sign themselves out and take a pass, but I know other teachers who don't allow any bathroom visits during workshop time or who tell readers they have to wait for when the teacher isn't conferring to give a hand signal that they need to use the bathroom.

To encourage stamina from my class, I teach them strategies for what to do when they get distracted or run out of steam. I teach them strategies like rereading to get back into the book, jotting Post-its at the end of each chapter to quickly retell what happened on that page, or even moving to a quieter spot free of distractions.

Supplies are always an issue, so I developed a system in my room where readers can troubleshoot these problems themselves. I have a place in the room where students can exchange their dull pencils for sharp ones so that quiet readers won't be distracted by the noise of pencil sharpeners. There is always a heaping pile of Post-it notes that students can borrow in a basket near the library.

I also have to decide what to do when, despite my best efforts, one of my students says, "I'm done!" or, "I don't have any Post-its!" In my classroom, I often have a visual reminder of what they are supposed to do. In some cases it is a chart with expectations recorded. This is often a document from a prior minilesson or teaching share. In other cases, there is a part of the room that is labeled in a self-explanatory way, so when a reader goes there she can figure it out independently. Often, I simply gesture to the basket with Post-its, or point to a chart that reads "What To Do When You Feel Finished with Your Reading." What I try to never do is to engage in a conversation with the student, as this interferes with independence and causes the student to be dependent on me to solve her problems.

During a Reading Workshop, a Reader Can . . .

- Read independently
- Jot notes on Post-its as you read
- Jot a note of something you want to share with a friend
- Take a Post-it from an independent reading book and write more about it in your notebook
- Reread something read before
- Sign out for a brief visit to the bathroom, if it really can't wait

During a Reading Workshop, a Reader May Not . . .

- Interrupt the teacher while conferring
- Interrupt another reader
- Do work for another subject area (like math)

Teach Students Their Roles When They're in a Conference

In order for me to meet with my readers with any frequency, it's essential that I get good at conferring quickly. A lot of what I discuss in Chapter 10 will help you to feel ready and prepared for conferences, but your students should also feel like they are prepared.

From the moment I sit down with a student, she should be aware of what her role is in a conference. I often decide to teach a whole-class minilesson where I discuss this role. I let my students know that when I sit down and ask them to tell me what's happening with their reading, they are expected to tell me not only about their books but also about their processes. It should become habit for the students to tell me brief summaries of the parts they're reading and also a bit about the strategies they're trying out, what they're struggling with, and what ideas they're having as they read. I also teach students that they should expect to be ready to show me evidence of how they've been trying out the strategies that I've taught them in the last few conferences we've had together, as well as strategies they've learned in whole-class minilessons if they were appropriate. I write more in Chapter 8, about holding students accountable for previous teaching.

Students also need to learn that there is a predictable structure to my conferences, as discussed in the last chapter. It helps when students know that, after we have a brief discussion about what they're reading, I'll teach them something that they'll be expected to try out. Knowing that my conferences follow a predictable structure helps them to know what to do.

Manage Yourself

It is helpful for me to think through some of the choreography of conferring. Specifically:

- Where am I going to confer;
- How can I stick to a schedule; and
- What will I be carrying with me?

In my classroom, I always find it helpful to go to a student to have a conference as opposed to having a student come to me. This technique is useful for a few reasons. For one, positioning myself physically in the room allows me to manage my class a little better. My presence is felt, and between conferences I can get up and move around the classroom to check in with students that I've had a conference with or with students who need refocusing or encouragement. In addition, I also find at times that what I am teaching one student can also help one or more of the other students at the table, and I can easily form a small-group conference. Students also often overhear conferences and try out in their own reading what I've taught one student.

Classroom Applications

- Decide on a predictable structure for your reading time. If you'll follow a reading workshop, you may want to look into other resources like *The Art of Teaching Reading* (Calkins 2001) where these structures are described in more detail.

- Create a classroom library that is clearly labeled and has a lot of books, a large portion of which are labeled with the reading level. Decide on a system for borrowing books that is fast and effective.

- Decide upon ways your students will write about their reading, and how they will keep track of the quantity and types of books they've read.

- Think about ways you'll explicitly teach students to be independent. Troubleshoot problems by thinking about what you can do proactively.

- Consider where you'll confer, what you'll need with you, and perhaps even a schedule to ensure you see everyone equitably.

Matching Students to Just-Right Books

"'Ahhh, this porridge is just right,' she said happily, and she ate it all up."

— GOLDILOCKS AND THE THREE BEARS

It happens to me every Monday morning: I look into my closet stuffed full of clothes and I complain, "I have nothing to wear." If you were to peer into the closet, you'd probably disagree. I have hanger after hanger of jeans (one pair, my "skinny jeans," haven't been on my body since the weather turned cold and I've gone back to eating comfort food as a regular practice), an entire folding-shelf system full of sweaters, dresses for when I need to attend a wedding or cocktail party, and shelves of shoes. I have button-down shirts, many of which are not ironed and ready to put on, and a high shelf stacked with boxes labeled according to sizes that I used to be and want to be again, and sizes that I used to be and never hope to be again. But most Mondays, it goes like this: I stand there frozen with my hands on my hips and a frown on my face, staring into the closet.

So what is it exactly that I'm looking for? I need something professional enough that it looks like I put some effort into getting dressed, yet something comfortable enough that I can get down on the floor with students in the many classrooms I'll visit that day. In the words of Goldilocks, I'm looking for an outfit that's "just right."

My job as a teacher, as early as the first day of school and continually across the entire year, is to help students feel comfortable as they read. I need to help them find books that they will feel are "just right"—books that they can read with fluency, accuracy, and comprehension. When I make the mistake of wearing a pair of pants that is too tight, I spend the day not only uncomfortable, but also self-conscious and feeling bad about myself. This feeling is exactly what I want to avoid with students' book choices. Pretending to read a book that's too hard could leave students feeling bad about themselves as readers.

Feeling "just right" isn't just about being cozy, though. Researchers like Richard Allington (2001) have shown that students need to read a lot, and they need to read books that they can read. Allington cites research that shows students who choose books they can read with less than ninety-seven percent accuracy show marked increases in off-task behaviors. As I think about myself as an adult reader, I know that when something is hard or frustrating, I often abandon it. It makes sense, then, that I wouldn't ask my students to spend hours a day feeling frustrated.

Just as I have my pair of "skinny jeans" that haven't been touched in a while, it's nice for students to have goals that they're working toward. Students, too, might have some more challenging books that they'll want to try on from time to time, but the majority of their time spent in independent reading should involve reading books that feel comfortable. And of all the clothes—or books—that fit, there are different times for different types. In my classroom, there is a time for students to read nonfiction, a time to read books with strong characters, and a time to read poetry.

When I first meet my students at the start of a new school year, I urgently work to find out about them as readers so I can help guide them in their own book choices. I work so that all students are matched to just-right books by the end of the first few weeks of school. And across the year, just as my clothing size seems to fluctuate and I take one of those boxes down from the top shelf and pack up some of the hanging clothes for later wear, so, too, do my readers change: their levels change, their interests change, and the class studies change. The type of conferences that I discuss in this chapter will help to guide students to just-right books. These conferences are meant to be done on the very first days of school and often throughout the year.

Getting Readers into Books Right Away

In the second half of this chapter, I discuss more formal assessments to be sure about our students' reading levels and their interests as readers. I don't want to send the message that independent reading should wait for those assessments to be completed! From day one of school, I introduce my classroom library to my students and have them choosing books.

Use Last Year's Assessment Data

If you teach in a school where there is a building-wide commitment to having students hold books they can read, chances are there is some system for communicating what a student's second-grade teacher knows to that student's future third-grade teacher. Many schools like this have a systematic form or card that travels with the cumulative record folder from one year to the next. On that card are the results of formal assessments, the student's end-of-year reading level, and some interests of the student. Figure 4-1 shows what such a form might look like.

Once I receive this form from last year's teacher, I often still need to do some adjustment. Frequently, readers who do not have ample opportunity to read over the summer can drop two or even three levels. Students who read moderately will remain at about the same level. And students who read voraciously can even increase levels over the two months of summer. Using what I know about their reading lives over the summer, I am able to place each reader in a probably-just-right level for the time being until I get to that student to assess his or her reading level more formally. If I'm not sure, I plan to err on the side of giving a student a book that's too easy because I don't want to encourage bad reading habits from the start. I don't want anyone to be disengaged, or to think that reading means struggling and being frustrated.

Teach Students the Three-Finger Rule

A very simple way to get my students independently monitoring their reading in books that are "just right" is to teach them the "three-finger rule." To do this, I teach students to read a page or two (depending on the density of text on the page), and put up a finger for each word they don't know (Allington 2001). If they hold up three fingers before reaching the end of their page, it means the text may be too hard. While this isn't always one hundred percent foolproof— it banks on the fact that the students will read about one hundred words in that page or two and that they actually know when they read a word incorrectly— it does serve as a quick way to get my students reading right away. In many

Name: _Joaquain Smith_____ From class: _3 - 304_

Student reading level: __M____ State Assessment (ELA): low 3

Books this student likes to read:

J.S. LOVES nonfiction — snakes, lizards, reptiles.
Disliked char. unit of study. Reads a lot of
Magic Tree House. Likes a lot of action, less
char. development

What is this student like in partnerships and clubs?

J.S. is great in partnerships. Is motivated when
he has a peer to "answer to!" Doesn't always
do reading @ home unless it's for partners or
clubs. He's a strong conversationalist.

Figure 4-1. A sample cross-grade articulation card.

cases, this means that it's a good rule for books at or above a level L or M (which includes popular series such as *Pinky and Rex*, *Magic Tree House*, and the *Polk Street Kids*). Books at lower levels have fewer words on the page, and therefore three errors would yield a much lower percentage accuracy rate.

I often teach this strategy for book choosing as one of my first minilessons, along with teaching students to stop at the end of the page or two and make sure they can tell themselves what happened in the part they just read to make sure they comprehend. Many students, and even some teachers, erroneously believe that if a student can *say* all the words on the page, then he is reading. I don't want to give my readers the impression that saying all the words is reading. Even saying all the words fluently and with expression isn't reading. Comprehension is essential. So when using this strategy, it's vital that I also talk to my students about the importance of monitoring for sense as a final check before finding a just-right book.

Assess Comprehension Quickly

One year, as a third-grade teacher, I did not have my students' reading levels at the beginning of the year. I was wary about letting all thirty-two of my students descend upon the classroom library equipped only with the three-finger strategy. I wanted to have a better assessment to approximate their reading levels as I met with each reader in the class, starting essentially from scratch trying to learn about them. I felt that if I had them holding books that were most likely at their approximate reading level, I could rest more assured that students were not wasting time with books that were too difficult.

I found a few books at levels that tend to be common in third grade, and chose one book at each level that I was sure was leveled correctly. I picked a *Poppleton* book by Cynthia Rylant for level J, a *Frog and Toad* book by Arnold Lobel for level K, *Pinky and Rex* by James Howe for level L, the *Magic Tree House* series by Mary Pope Osborne for level M, and *The Stories Julian Tells* by Ann Cameron for level N. (Some teachers I work with prefer to use less familiar texts just so they ensure that the students haven't seen or read them before. This is a great idea if you have access to them, but I didn't.) I got a few copies of each title so I could have them ready to hand out. I asked each student to tell me the titles of the last books she remembered reading. I then asked her to read the first chapter of a book that was one level below the book she mentioned. After talking to each student, they all had a book in their hands. I told them to read their chapter carefully, and when they were done to please write a retelling on separate blank piece of paper without looking back at the chapters. I did this because I wanted to make sure that my assessment matched what students actually would do during independent reading. If they had the opportunity during an assessment to look back a dozen times, then this would not give me an assessment of what they normally did.

As students read and wrote, I moved around the room. When I noticed a student seemed to be having a hard time writing, I pulled her aside and asked her to tell me the story orally. The writing of the retelling was only a time-saver—if a student was able to retell a story orally but had trouble writing, I accommodated the assessment for her because it was an assessment of her reading comprehension, not her writing ability. If I noticed students seeming disengaged, I asked them to stop and quickly tell what happened in their chapters so far, and if they were unable to do so I gave them copies of easier texts to try. I did the same once the students started to write their retellings—if I noticed students had many inaccuracies in their retellings, I stopped them and handed them easier texts. It was important that I didn't make this feel punitive; I said something like "Great job with that! Let's give this next one a try." If a student breezed through a text (reading faster than two hundred words per minute) and seemed to have no trouble with the retelling, I tried that student with a harder text. To determine this reading rate, I sometimes timed the student reading a page. Students that breezed through their chapters but struggled with the retellings then received easier chapters because comprehension was essential. By the end of the first day, I had a good estimation of most of the students' levels, and I felt more comfortable beginning my more-formal assessments. If I was still unsure, I preferred to err on the side of matching readers to books that were too easy, because my goal in the very start of the year was to get students engaged and to help them feel comfortable with reading. This method was not the most foolproof method, but it was a nice quick way to get a general sense of the classroom at the start. Even after doing a more-informal assessment, I knew it was still important to assess the readers in my class using more-formal methods, which are described in the next section.

QUICK ASSESSMENT TO GET STUDENTS INTO BOOKS RIGHT AWAY

- Use information from last year's teachers.
- Teach students to independently use the "three-finger" rule to find books they can read at ninety-seven percent accuracy on their own.
- Give students at higher reading levels book chapters and ask them to write retellings.

Assessing Formally

Once I have my students settled into books that are close enough to their real just-right level and they can stay engaged for sustained periods of time, I am freed up to do confer with readers. In the next sections, I describe conferences with readers to administer running records to assess for accuracy, fluency, and comprehension; the reading inventory to learn about reading interests and attitudes; and research-only conferences to learn about readers' processes and strategies.

The Running Record

Running records were made mainstream by Marie Clay as a way to record what students do as you sit and listen to them read. This section briefly explains how to do a running record, but I recommend reading *Running Records for Classroom Teachers* (Clay 2000) for more detailed help.

The purpose of doing a running record is two-fold. First, I want to make sure that I know at what levels students are able to read with high degrees of accuracy, fluency, and comprehension. I also want to do running records to begin to develop ideas about ways to work with students in conferences to figure out what skills and processes to reinforce and what to teach.

Figure 4-2.

A running record is an opportunity for me to listen to a student read, to take notes on when he makes an error or "miscue," and to listen for fluency and intonation, an accurate retelling, and correct answers to inference questions. I can analyze these records to see what students do when they run into difficulty. I ask myself, what errors do they make and why? When, if at all, do they self-correct? How fluently do they read?

When taking a running record, I record the miscues or errors a reader makes as he reads a new text aloud. Typically, I ask a student to read only about one to two hundred words aloud. If a student is reading books where there are less than one hundred words, I listen to the entire book. As the student reads, I write down what he reads and all of his reading behaviors. Because the reading happens quickly, I use a shorthand developed by Clay (2000) for taking these notes.

Clay's shorthand is summarized in the chart on page 39. When a student reads a word correctly, a checkmark is recorded. When a reader attempts (by sounding out or repeating sounds), those attempts are recorded on top of a line and the word from the text is recorded below. This is not recorded as an error but can be analyzed later. If a student deletes a word, the teacher records a dash above the line with the word from the text on the bottom, and when a student inserts a word that is not actually in the text, the word that the student says goes above a line with a dash below it.

Students may exhibit other reading behaviors as well. Sometimes, a student will appeal for help: This is recorded as an "A" on the top of the line because it is a student behavior. If the teacher tells the student the word, the teacher records a "T" on the bottom of the line because it is not a student behavior. When students self-correct, the teacher records an "SC" on the top line, right next to the original miscue. It's also important to record when students reread a word, a phrase, or an entire line, as well as the number of times it's repeated. If a phrase or word is repeated, the teacher draws a sweeping arrow over whatever is reread. Next to the arrow, the teacher will write "R" with the number (for example, "R2" means "repeat twice") to indicate the number of times that part was reread.

Some teachers choose a set of "benchmark books" (like the ones I mentioned earlier to assess comprehension) in order to start running records. The benefit of using a benchmark book is that I'm familiar with the book. Knowing the book makes it easier to take the running record and easier to listen for a correct

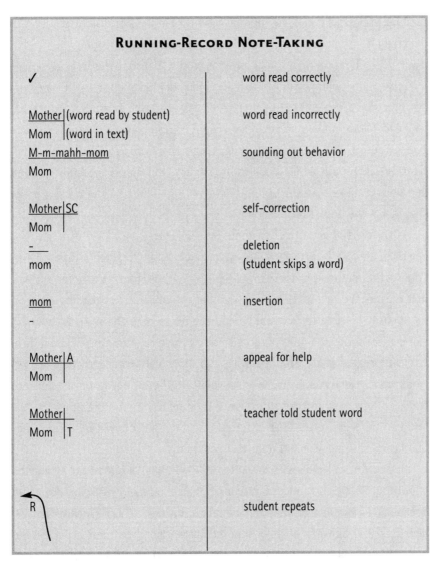

RUNNING-RECORD NOTE-TAKING

✓	word read correctly
Mother|(word read by student) Mom |(word in text)	word read incorrectly
M-m-mahh-mom Mom	sounding out behavior
Mother|SC Mom |	self-correction
‒ mom	deletion (student skips a word)
mom -	insertion
Mother|A Mom |	appeal for help
Mother| Mom |T	teacher told student word
R	student repeats

Adapted from Clay, 2000.

retelling at the end of recording the miscues. When I do running records this way, I can hand the book to the student and take notes on her reading on a separate sheet of paper or in a notebook. Some teachers who are newer to taking running records go a step further and type up a few hundred words of the text that the students are expected to read so they can take their notes on actual copies of the text as opposed to blank paper. Once I became more practiced, I started taking running records as part of my normal conferring routine by asking students to read right from the books they had chosen for independent reading.

To begin the running record, I have the reader sit next to me and I say something like, "I'm going to ask you to read a little out loud and then a little to yourself, and then at the end of this chapter, I'll ask you some questions about what you read. Please make sure you read it carefully, and go back to reread if you're ever confused, like you would do normally when you read independently." Next, I read the title of the book to the student and then I get ready to listen and write. I make sure I'm sitting next to the student so I can peer over her shoulder at the book as she reads.

As she reads, I record a checkmark for each correct word. When a new line begins in the text, I start a new line on my page. When the reader turns a page, I draw a line all the way across my paper. The purpose for taking notes in a way that mirrors the text is that when I go back to analyze her reading later, I'll more easily be able to find the part in the text where the miscue occurred. Having this contextual information is important in determining what kinds of error the student made. Students will predictably read words incorrectly; insert words that aren't there; delete words that are there; repeat words, lines, or entire sentences; sound out words when they are having trouble; appeal to you for help; and self-correct their own mistakes. I try to get down all the information I can using a consistent note-taking system.

I learned from Kathleen Tolan at the TCRWP that it's important to take the opportunity not only to record miscues, but also to record what I notice about a reader's fluency and intonation. She taught me to do this by having the student read the first one to two hundred words aloud to track accuracy and record miscues, and the next one hundred words to record fluency. When I do this, I shift my attention away from listening for the exact words a student reads and instead I focus on where I hear breaks, pauses, or repetition. When I have a typed copy of the text, I just mark in between the words with a forward slash, and when I am taking a record on a blank sheet of paper I mark the forward slash in between checkmarks. It's also important to note what readers do with punctuation. I mark down places where the student reads through punctuation where she should otherwise stop or pause (commas, periods). I also record whether the student is able to read dialogue with intonation; there should be a distinct difference between the way a student reads narration and dialogue.

Figure 4-3 is an example of a running record where the purpose of the first one hundred words was to record miscues, in Marie Clay's format. During the second one hundred words, I took notes on fluency and intonation.

If I notice that the student is making many errors, like Amar in Figure 4-3, or that the student's reading is disfluent (it is choppy—one or two words at a time and doesn't sound smooth like it does when she talks), then that is an indication that the text is not an appropriate level. When looking at miscues, it is important to know that the goal is for the student to be able to read with about ninety-seven-percent accuracy, meaning no more than three errors for every one hundred words. I do not count misread proper names as an error, and repeated words that the reader miscues on more than once only count as one error. It's also important to consider a reader's oral language proficiency; I do not expect perfect reading fluency from students who, because of language difficulties or because they are learning English as a second language, don't speak fluently.

If fluency or accuracy is affected, I stop the running record at this point because it can be very time consuming to listen to a student struggle through several levels, recording errors as I go. It's also frustrating and humiliating for the student.

After the student has read, I then have him either stop and retell what he has read, or I have him read to the end of the chapter silently and then ask him to retell what he has read. When I listen to the retelling, I want to be sure that the student recounts the important events of the story in the order in which they happened. If the retelling is sparse, I assess for literal comprehension by asking questions whose answers can be found in the text, such as:

- Please retell what you just read. How did it start?
- Who is . . . ?
- What is . . . ?
- What happened after . . . ?

I then ask some inferential comprehension questions, or questions where the student will have to think about the information in the text and have her own thoughts or ideas:

- How do you think the character felt at this point?
- Why did the character do what he did?
- What kind of person is this character?

Amar   11/15/07   (Level K)

Fox
"Fox, dear," said Fox's mom.

"Just where do you think you ~~are going~~?"   go isc R

"Out to have fun with the gang," said Fox.

"It's Saturday."

"But today you must take care of little Louise," said Mom.

kidding
"You're ~~joking~~," said Fox.

"I am *not* joking!" said Mom.

And she gave Fox a look.

"Come on, Louise," said Fox.

Fox went to see his friend Dexter. But Dexter's mom came to the door.

"Sorry, Fox," she said.

"Dexter has to help at home all day."

"That's no fun," said Fox.

"Come on, Louise."

watch for
Dexter ~~watched from~~ the window.

"Sorry, Fox," he said.

Next

----100 words----

Fox went to Betty's house/ "Betty has chicken pox," said her mom.

ignored → "Can she still play?" asked Fox.

ignored → "Of course not," said Betty's mom.

"Poor Betty" said Fox/

ignored → Come on/ Louise/

"Okay," said Louise/

ignored → Sorry, Fox said Betty/

"You can't help it," said Fox/

Figure 4-3.

If the student has read with ninety-seven-percent or higher accuracy, his reading is fluent, and his comprehension is evident based on his retelling or follow-up comprehension questions, then I've found that student's "just-right," or independent, reading level. Then, I have the student go to the classroom library and choose a few books at that level. If any one of these three conditions is shaky, I find a lower level and do a new running record. If a student seems to read every word correctly and is able to do deeper comprehension work, I try a harder level.

After taking a running record, I have not only found a reader's independent reading level, but I also have a sense of the way he handles difficulty in books. When you get ready to use this data to inform your instruction, see Chapter 10, where you can find more detailed help with analyzing this data.

Administering running records as a conference, then, follows a very predictable structure that differs from the research-decide-teach conference that is described in later chapters. It is an essential type of conference to do at the beginning of the year, and across the year, as I work to match students to just-right books and continually strive to know them better as readers.

STEPS TO TAKING A RUNNING RECORD

- Have a student copy and a teacher copy of a benchmark text (or blank page for teacher notes).
- Decide on your shorthand system—Marie Clay's or your own.
- Listen to the student read aloud and record what you hear.
- Jot down notes about the student's fluency and intonation.
- Ask the student comprehension questions to assess literal and inferential comprehension.
- Try an easier level if the student didn't read fluently with ninety-seven-percent accuracy, or if she is not able to answer comprehension questions.
- Try a harder level if the student demonstrates that there are no areas of challenge and can answer higher-level inference comprehension questions with ease.

The Reading Inventory

Reading levels are just one part of getting to know my students as readers. It is also important to find out what they like to read, their history as readers, and their attitudes about reading. The reading inventory can be an invaluable tool for gathering this information.

Reading inventories can be done as either conferences or questionnaires. Some teachers may consider asking questions during an initial conference with readers either before or after they've listened to them read and they've done running records. Sometimes I had my students complete these questionnaires for homework because I was trying to save time. I often was frustrated, though, at the lesser quality of their responses. Then, I started instead to have students work on them in class while I worked on assessing my class using running records.

My first questionnaires asked such questions as:

- What kind of books do you like to read?
- Who is your favorite author?
- What kind of books does your family read to you at home?
- Do you like to read stories and/or do you like to read books where you learn cool facts?

But then Donna Santman, author of *Shades of Meaning* (2005), taught me that this type of inventory is really an opportunity to uncover difficulty, struggles, and resistance. I then started asking questions about times when reading felt like a struggle, times when students felt unsuccessful as readers, and books that they didn't enjoy. I also changed such questions as "What kind of books do you like to read?" to more open-ended questions that didn't make as many assumptions, such as:

- What do you feel when you hear "It's time to read!" in school?
- Are there any books that you enjoy reading?

The second set of questions does not make the same assumptions that the first did—that is, that the student considers himself to be a reader and has had positive reading experiences. The phrasing of the second set ideally sets me up to get more honest answers.

The information I glean from these interviews or questionnaires helps me to direct students toward the areas in the library where they will be more successful in finding books in which they're more likely to be engaged, helps me to assign them reading partners, and angles my future conferences with the them.

Research-Only Conferences

Research-only conferences are always rare in my classroom because I want to take most opportunities to give compliments or teach something new before I move on to a new student. There are, however, a few specific instances when I choose to do them: first, when I'm initially getting to know my students and I want to get some information about the strategies they use when they read to help me to get ready for my conferences; second, when I'm working to manage a class and can't afford to sit for many minutes with one student, I may choose to do research-only conferences because they allow me to move around the room quickly; and third, when I'm trying to sort my students to plan for small-group conferences, I do short research-only conferences in order to quickly place my readers into a few groups.

In these conferences, I move quickly around the room, observing and asking questions to learn a little about the students' reading processes. I sometimes hang back to observe, trying to notice apparent behaviors that are telling of deeper reading processes. I ask myself such questions as:

- Is the student staying on one page for a very long time?
- Is the student pointing to the words or moving his mouth when she reads?
- How much time does the student spend looking around the room instead of reading his book?

Sometimes, I simply go over to a student and ask questions about what he's doing as a reader. I might ask a student to show me some of the Post-its he's written, or to walk me through some of the writing in his reading notebook. I may also ask a few open-ended questions, such as, "What's going on in this part of your book?", "Can you tell me a little about the characters in your book?", or, if the book is nonfiction, "What are you learning about right now?" I jot down the precious information the student gives me in my notes—either a class list checklist/grid or forms that are individual for each student.

Checklist for Research-Only Conferences																					
Names																					
Finger-pointing																					
Mouthing words																					
Looking around room																					
Using Post-its for retelling																					
Using Post-its for ideas																					
Exhibiting engaged behaviors																					

Above is one example of such a form. See Chapter 12 for more guidance on establishing your own note-taking system.

Getting to know a whole class of new readers and setting them up to be independent and successful in their books can seem like a daunting challenge. I always want to keep it a goal in my classroom to get students into books fast, and I have found a few methods to help with fast matching—namely, using last year's data, teaching students the three-finger rule, and having them write brief retellings of chapters of books that I know well. Of course, I always want to check back in on these less-exact assessment measures, and I try to complete a running record on every student in my class within the first few weeks of school. Keeping in mind that a level is only one aspect of a reader, I make sure also to have interviews or hand out questionnaires to get to know my students' interests and passions so that I can put books in their hands that they are sure to love.

Classroom Applications

■ Make it your goal to help readers find books they will feel successful with as early in the school year as possible. Plan out how you will conduct quick assessments from the very first days of the school year.

■ Consider multiple approaches to getting information about your students as readers. Students are more than just reading levels. They have histories with books, attitudes about reading, and passions that are waiting to be uncovered. Learn about them through conferences that get at their reading behaviors and processes.

■ Teach readers trying out books with more than one hundred words per page to monitor their accuracy by trying the "three-finger" rule.

■ Encourage your school to have a building-wide plan for communicating information about your readers from one grade to the next. This plan may be a communication form on which you might include information about their reading levels as well as the kinds of reader that you have found them to be. This information will help the students' subsequent teachers to match them to books quickly.

5 Reinforcing Students' Strengths: Compliment Conferences

"They kissed his wet pink nose. They admired his small black eyes.
And they stroked his sweet white fur.
'Julius is the baby of the world,' chimed Lilly's parents."

— Julius the Baby of the World, by Kevin Henkes

For weeks I observed Linh, a third grader, struggle to keep track of the main events across the chapters in her books. When she began reading a new chapter, she often forgot what happened in the previous chapters and found herself either confused or rereading entire chapters to get herself back on track. One day I sat next to Linh and asked her about her Amber Brown book. She showed me two Post-its: one at the end of Chapter 1 and another at the end of Chapter 2. Linh explained that at the end of every chapter, she jotted down notes about what happened in the chapter to help her remember. I read her Post-it notes and realized she was writing entire summaries on them. While I wanted to teach Linh how to take notes in more efficient ways by just jotting down a few words, during this conference I decided to reinforce this new strategy she was already using. "Linh," I began, "I love how you jotted down some notes at the end of every chapter to remind yourself of the main events. This will help you remember the previous chapters as you begin reading new ones." I continued by describing her strategy step by step and encouraging her to keep using the strategy as long as it continued to help her. Linh nodded and continued reading.

Why Start with Students' Strengths

For many important reasons, my colleagues and I at the TCRWP usually start off each school year focusing on what the readers in our rooms already do well by reinforcing their strengths as readers and noticing their approximations. Lucy Calkins and colleagues describe these compliment conferences in *One to One* (2005) and the *Units of Study for Writing* sets (2003 and 2006) as ways to deepen students' current approximations of strategies. One reason I start by complimenting is that it sets the tone for the rest of the year by showing students I am a teacher who notices strengths. In addition, I know that many students (and adults for that matter) are more likely to take risks in their learning when they feel safe and competent already. I want the students in my classroom to see themselves as strong readers with lots to offer the rest of our reading community. This confidence will help them take risks later on in the school year. Also, I know that one of the best ways to get students to use consistently the strategies that they currently may use only occasionally is to compliment their use of the strategy. Finally, I can work more frequently with each student if I sit with her for only a minute or two to give a compliment in order to get to know each student well.

WHY START WITH STUDENTS' STRENGTHS

- It sets a positive tone where students know their strengths are recognized.
- It helps foster an environment where students are willing to take risks.
- It encourages students to use consistently strategies they already are able to do or are just beginning to approximate.
- It allows me to work with students more frequently.

The Role of Complimenting in a Conference

A full teaching conference is one that follows the typical structure of a reading conference—research the reader, decide what to compliment and teach, and teach the reader. A compliment conference is often shorter and only includes the research and decision phase. The decision is what to compliment and reinforce. While the compliment is a small part of every conference, it can also be an entire conference on its own. When complimenting, I choose something important to reinforce by specifically naming a strategy and complimenting the student for using it.

The decision phase is important because I tend to compliment strategies that are new or emerging. I don't compliment strategies that are already a part of the reader's typical reading behaviors because that does not deepen the student's reading. Instead, I compliment a strategy that the reader is just learning to approximate so she will continue using it more frequently.

I am likely to have compliment conferences when I notice students' reading stamina is low, students are unfocused during independent reading, students are unwilling or afraid to take risks, students' motivation and energy levels seem low, or when students are not consistently using strategies they already know how to do.

Many teachers also choose to have compliment conferences while they are learning to confer. By just focusing on the research and compliment—the first few minutes of a full-length conference—it helps to learn the qualities of a good compliment and to manage a class of children who may be new to sustaining their own independent reading. When I choose to have compliment conferences, they tend to take the form of two structures: individual-compliment conferences and table-compliment conferences.

Individual Compliment Conferences

Individual compliment conferences are short—about two minutes—and involve researching the reader and giving a compliment. In compliment conferences I do not teach a new strategy; instead, I reinforce a strategy the reader is already beginning to use. While I see the need to constantly push my students to grow as readers by teaching them new and increasingly more sophisticated strategies, I also believe in the value of making sure some strategies consistently are being used with independence. Taking this time to reinforce the use of a strategy will often yield greater benefits in the long run when I ask the reader to take a risk with something more challenging or brand new.

Researching with a Lens of Strengths

It can be difficult for me to notice what students are doing well and is often easier for me to notice what I wish they were doing differently. I use both observation and conversation as methods of research to figure out what the reader already is trying to do. I constantly force myself to look for strengths and evidence of strategies that the reader is using already. I sometimes think to myself, "What should this reader be proud of?" or "What is this reader showing me she knows how to do?"

Using Observation to Look for Individual Students' Strengths

The most important aspect of researching readers for compliment conferences is the ability to step back and observe students reading while looking for what they are doing. For some reason, I always notice first the kinds of things students are not doing. It is almost as if I have "teacher radar" that points me toward misbehaviors and unfocused readers. I am sure I am not alone in this trait. But, when I decide to start with students' strengths, I force myself to adjust my radar, to put on new teacher lenses and begin looking for what students already are doing well. As I observe readers I think to myself, "What is this reader doing well that seems new and important?" Sometimes it takes only a few seconds to notice strong reading behaviors, but on other days—like Halloween or the day before a long break, for example—it takes some time and patience to notice something positive to reinforce.

Starting my observation from afar helps me find possible compliments as students transition into independent reading. I learned from Colleen Cruz, a colleague and author of *Independent Writing* (2004), the benefits of observing students from near and afar. Observation from afar means I usually stand by my meeting area, pick up my conferring clipboard, and instantly begin asking myself, "Who are the model readers today?" I usually am able to find at least one student to compliment during the transition from my whole-class minilesson in the meeting area to independent reading. There is always at least one reader who quickly, quietly, and efficiently gathers his materials and begins reading.

Often, after my first compliment conference is completed (about two minutes into the independent reading time), the students are focused on reading.

At this point, I adjust my observations to include near observation. When I use near observation with readers, I tend to stand behind them as they read. I watch their facial expressions to look for engagement. I glance at what they are writing on their Post-its or jotting in their reading notebooks.

In this near observation, I am looking for as much evidence of strong reading behaviors as possible. The kinds of strategies I notice tend to fall into a few categories: strategies for staying focused and engaged, strategies that were previously taught in minilessons and conferences, or new strategies that make me say, "Wow." I notice what strategies students are using to stay focused and engaged in their books. This might be turning a chair away from the others, as in Billy's case, or Sonia's choosing to read a few books from the reading series she loves. I also notice what strategies students are using that were taught in whole-class minilessons or conferences. For example, if I taught my fourth-grade class to jot down the clues on Post-it notes as they read their mystery books or I taught my first graders to point under every word as they read, I could use these strategies as potential compliments. These categories helped me to refine my radar to look for reading models.

KINDS OF NEAR OBSERVATION FOR POSSIBLE COMPLIMENTS

- Strategies for staying focused and engaged in reading
- Strategies that were previously taught
- Strategies that students "invent"
- Strategies that students are just beginning to approximate and use

---

I may choose to start with far observation of a reader if I want to research the reader's engagement and routines. But, if these are not problems, I may choose to skip far observation and begin by standing closely behind the reader. All my research decisions are based on what I know about the reader. For example, if I know that Thinh is always the first reader to get his book out and begin reading, I do not need to observe his transition; instead, I walk right up to him and observe. Likewise, if I know that Thomas rarely has Post-its in his books and often has nothing prepared to say during partner talk time, I may observe Thomas from afar to see how long it takes him to get started reading, whether he keeps Post-its on his desk while he reads, and how much he is reading versus daydreaming. Whether I observe from afar and near or not, I make sure to take a few seconds to one minute to observe the reader and notice what he is already able to do.

Having a Conversation to Look for Students' Strengths

There are times when quickly observing the reader gives me plenty of ideas for what I could compliment and reinforce, but there are other readers with whom I need to spend more time. For many readers, I learn a lot from talking to them about their thinking. I usually ask the reader to describe her process and thinking while I notice what she is already able to do. I may start by asking something like, "What are you thinking about right now?" If the student has Post-it notes or if I have been teaching many strategies around a specific skill, I may ask more focused questions, such as, "Can you show me a place where you made a strong picture in your mind?" Or I may look at a Post-it and say, "Can you tell me why you put this Post-it here and how this helped you?" These questions are not meant as a quiz, but as a means for me to get a better picture of the reader's strengths. If I notice the reader is struggling in this conversation, I move on so that I don't focus my attention on strategies the reader *could* use. I want to focus on what the reader already is doing well.

Giving Compliments That Reinforce Strategies

Once I finish my research and pinpoint a strategy the reader is already doing well, I begin giving a compliment that will reinforce the consistent use of the strategy. I follow a similar structure so that I keep it short and simple. I describe a specific example of the reader's strategy, then I tell the reader why the strategy is helpful. Finally, I state the steps of the strategy in a way that makes it transferable to all books.

After researching Lacey by using near observation and having a brief conversation, I decided to compliment her on her use of rereading when she gets confused. I began by describing what I saw Lacey doing. "Lacey," I said with a smile, "I am so proud of the way you were reading your book. I noticed that when you were reading this paragraph where Junie B. was talking to her teacher, who she calls *Mrs.* you got confused. But you didn't just keep reading. Instead you went back and reread that part again so that you could figure out who was speaking and what they were saying to each other." I proceeded to tell her why this was a good strategy. "It is always a good idea to stop and reread places that are confusing. Readers like you know that reading needs to make sense, and, when it doesn't make sense, you need to go back and try again." Finally, I restated the steps of the strategy in a way that was transferable to all books. "Lacey, I really want you to remember to keep using this strategy: to notice when something does not makes sense or gets confusing, to stop and reread that section, and to make sure you understand the section before moving on. Great job and keep it up!" I stood up to leave as Lacey nodded with pride.

STRUCTURE OF INDIVIDUAL-COMPLIMENT CONFERENCES

- Research the reader through observation and conversation looking for strengths.
- Choose the strategy you want to reinforce.
- Give a specific example of when the reader used the strategy.
- Tell the reader why this strategy is helpful.
- Restate the steps of the strategy in a way that transfers to all books and explain the context for when the strategy will be useful again.

Table Compliment Conferences

While compliment conferences are often something I do on an individual basis, I also use this structure with a small group of readers at the same time. Kathleen Tolan taught me that the structure and purposes for table-compliment conferences are similar to individual-compliment conferences. Table-compliment conferences are used during times in the year when all the students in my class need support that day. This is typically in the beginning of the school year, after school vacations, and when the normal school schedule is altered. Table-compliment conferences allow me to move quickly around the classroom, get to every table of readers, and help them use strategies to focus on their reading. In most cases I use the table conference to either notice something the whole table of readers is doing well and reinforce it, or to notice something one reader is doing well and compliment it in a way that shows other readers at the table how to use the strategy. I remember the time Patrick invented a strategy where he made up symbols to remember his thinking and jotted them on Post-its. This new strategy, Patrick's strategy, became a table compliment where I taught all the readers at the table how to read like Patrick.

Giving Table Compliments Based on One Model Reader

I typically begin the research phase of the table conference by doing both far and near observations of an entire table of readers. Then I decide what to compliment and quickly move into giving the compliment to a model reader in a way that shows other readers at the table how they can do the same. This happens in a predictable way—I compliment one reader and ask the rest of the readers to try the strategy. I try to stay consistent in the way I give the compliments so the readers know what to expect and also so I can keep them short and to the point.

I almost always move from observing to asking for the whole table's attention. I tend to say something like, "Can all readers at this table close their books please and put their eyes on me? Thanks." This ensures I am not just talking to the student who was already employing the strategy, but using this table conference as an opportunity to teach all the readers at the table. Once I have everyone's attention, I begin giving the compliment. The compliment is not just one quick sentence, but about a "paragraph of talking," as Kathleen has taught me, that includes a description of the specific strategy, the reason why this was helpful, and a restatement of the strategy's steps so all the readers can try it.

As a staff developer, I often demonstrate conferences and support teachers while they have them. I remember coaching Ms. Ali on a rainy October afternoon as she observed Table 2 in her first-grade classroom. She stood back and began far observation of the table and smiled as she noticed all the readers at the table were holding books, reading in quiet voices, and attempting to point under the words. She moved closer and began near observation by crouching down behind a few readers, listening and watching as they read, and then moving around the table until she was back behind the student she began with. I noticed she paused a few seconds longer behind Jamal, but she still managed to observe every reader quickly. She moved to a space between chairs at the table and said, "Will you all please put your books down and give me your attention?" Each reader did as he or she was asked, and Ms. Ali continued: "I want to share something with all of you that I noticed Jamal doing. I noticed that when Jamal was reading and he got to a new, hard word in his book, he didn't just give up and skip the word." She picked up the book and turned to the page where Jamal used the strategy. "Instead, he looked at the picture and saw a monkey, then he looked at the first letters of the word and saw the letter *m* and said 'mmm' to make sure the word *monkey* matched the beginning letters of the word. Finally, he reread the whole sentence to make sure the word *monkey* would make sense. He read: 'I see a monkey.'" The other students watched as Ms. Ali gave this brief description of Jamal's strategy and demonstrated the steps.

Ms. Ali knew that she would have to make this strategy more generalizable to all books, not just Jamal's, so that the other readers at the table could benefit from this compliment conference. "This was so smart of Jamal," she continued. "It was a good idea for Jamal to try a few things to figure out this hard word because readers do not just try one thing and give up. They try everything they can think of to figure out a hard word." This elevated Jamal's status as the model reader and made him grin ear to ear. I wished I could have taken his photo, one of his two front teeth missing and all, and written the words "great reader" next to it.

Ms. Ali made sure to say a few more sentences that would restate Jamal's strategy so the others could begin using it. "So do you all think you could be like Jamal?" The others at the table nodded. "Okay, then from now on when you get to a new, hard word in your books, you can be like Jamal. You can look at the picture and think about what word would make sense. Then you can look at the first letters and make sure they match the word you are saying. Finally, you can reread the whole sentence and make sure that word does make sense. Thanks for teaching us this, Jamal." Ms. Ali smiled and walked to the next table as the readers picked up their books and began reading again.

It is important that I kept track of these quick compliment conferences as I would any other conference. Doing so helped me to remember the strategies that each reader in my class was gesturing toward using with increased independence so that I could follow up in future individual or group conferences. But perhaps the most important reason for keeping track of who's been complimented is to ensure that everyone is complimented at some point. I always wanted to make sure that each student in my class felt as though he was an expert on some strategy, or at least felt validated and noticed for his efforts. This went a long way to not only reinforce reading habits and behaviors, but also to create a classroom in which we all learned from one another.

MAKING ONE READER THE MODEL

- Observe the readers for strengths, thinking, "Who could be the model reader?"
- Choose one reader's strategy to compliment.
- Stop the whole table and get everyone's attention.
- Describe the reader's strategy step by step.
- Explain why the strategy is helpful.
- Restate the steps of the strategy in a way that makes it transferable to all books.
- Ask all the readers to try the strategy and thank the model reader.
- Keep track of who's been made the model.

Giving Table Compliments to a Whole Table

Sometimes, and I am always proud on these days, I observe a table and notice that every single reader at the table could be the model reader. Instead of moving to a different table and leaving them alone, I tend to give a table compliment, making sure to elevate every reader at the table to model-reader status. I still observe and notice what I could compliment, but then I give the compliment in a way that reinforces everyone's use of a strong strategy. I describe what I observed, tell them why it was smart, and then remind them to keep using this strategy all the time.

About two days into my second-grade whole-class study of nonfiction books, I realized the students loved to read nonfiction. They lingered over diagrams and charts and then read the text on the page to figure out how it went together. They "oohed" and "ahhed" when they learned new and interesting information. On the third day of this study, I began my far observation and noticed every single reader was focused and engaged. The energy in the room was electric and I had to fight the urge to stop, sit down in my chair, and just let them do their thing. There are teachers who would have done just that. They claim that stopping students while they are engaged gets them off task. While this may be true for some students, I also knew that my students were used to the routine of being stopped briefly for conferences. Because this was the routine for independent reading, they knew it would happen; they also knew how to get back into their books once the conferences were done. So I did not just relish their engagement; I decided to do some near observation and compliment tables in order to reinforce strong reading strategies.

I approached a group of readers who were sitting on the floor with a basket of different bug books between them. Each reader was reading a different book about bugs, each reader had a Post-it handy, and each reader was making some sort of facial expression that looked like a cross between amazement and being grossed out. I sat down behind Wonbo, watched him take his Post-it note off his lap, and jot down the word "cool" on it. Then he placed the Post-it on top of the photo of what a bee's stinger looks like under a microscope. I scooted behind Thomas and watched him turn back to a page in his book that had a Post-it note with an exclamation point on it. The note was sticking to a diagram of some sort of water bug that was walking across the water. I moved behind the other two students in this area and then stopped to give my compliment. "Can everyone please put their books down and put their eyes on me?" I asked. I waited a few seconds and reminded Thomas a second time to put his book down. I said, "I know you all love your books and want to get back to reading, so I am just going to take two minutes to tell you all the smart things I saw you doing. Then you can get back to reading." Thomas put his book down and sat up taller when I put my hand on his shoulder.

I began by describing what I saw all of the readers at the table doing. I tried to describe their strategy in a way that incorporated what every reader in the group was doing. "I am so excited because when I was watching you all read, I noticed a strategy you were all using." Now I had noticed that different readers in this group used the strategy in varying degrees, but I acted as if they were all equally proficient. "Every one of you found places in your books where you learned something new and interesting from the pictures and put a Post-it on that part so that you could share it with your partner during partner time. You also wrote a word or symbol on the Post-it so you would remember why you marked that picture." I held up a few books to show them the Post-it notes.

After describing the strategy, I told them why this was something clever to keep doing. "You are all so smart to use the pictures in your nonfiction books—whether they are photographs, diagrams, or charts—to learn new information. The pictures in nonfiction books are so full of information, and taking the time to study them will teach you so much." They all had smiles and I noticed Thomas' was the broadest. "I also love that you put a Post-it note on top of pictures that were especially cool or interesting so that you would remember to share them with your partners. This will help you become a better partner who can quickly share new information."

Now that I had told them why their strategy was so great, I made sure to let them know they should keep using it. "So from now on, will you all keep using this strategy: looking carefully at the pictures, noticing when you learn something new and cool, and then marking those parts with a Post-it note to share with a partner during talk time?" I saw four nodding heads. As I stood up to walk away, Thomas was the first one to pick up his book and begin reading with a Post-it in hand.

USING THE WHOLE TABLE AS THE MODEL

- Observe the readers for strengths, thinking, "What are these readers doing well?"
- Choose a strategy that every reader is approximating to compliment.
- Stop the whole table and get everyone's attention.
- Describe the strategy step by step.
- Explain why the strategy is helpful in a way that shows the context of when to use the strategy again.

I used to say, "I already taught him to do this, but he keeps forgetting," or "She could do this last week, but she isn't doing it anymore." I often grew frustrated when readers do not continue using strategies that I already taught. Both individual-compliment conferences and table conferences offer me another chance to reinforce strategies that students are already able to use or just starting to approximate. Compliment conferences are also a great way to build confidence in readers. After all, when I get a compliment on a new skirt, I always tend to wear it more often. Students aren't that different from me—the more I notice and compliment strategies, the more likely they are to keep using them.

Classroom Applications

■ Practice observing students from afar and near. Jot down notes about what students are able to do or trying to do.

■ Practice having conversations with readers about their strategies and look for what students are approximating.

■ Keep a written or mental checklist in your head of the parts of a compliment conference. Remember to describe the strategy's steps, explain why it is useful, and make it transferable. These three parts will help the compliment "stick" with readers.

■ Try both individual and table compliment conferences. Move around the classroom thinking, "Who could be the model reader(s) at this table?" Make a point of making every reader a "model" at some point in the month.

Supporting Students During Whole-Class Studies

> "We've taught you that the earth is round,
> That red and white make pink,
> And something else that matters more—
> We've taught you how to think."
>
> — HOORAY FOR DIFFENDOOFER DAY!, BY DR. SEUSS

As the students walked into the classroom on Monday morning, their eyes grew big as they said, "Cool!" or "Wow!" The students' classroom library had been transformed to match the current whole-class study. The top shelf of the bookcases displayed poetry anthologies and collections. New baskets of books with poets' names and topics lined the second shelves. A chart stand was placed in the corner of the library with a few pages worth of class favorites written on them. "I can't wait to start reading poetry!" Tonya said to her classmate Donyea. "I know!" she replied. The students were ready to embark on a new study together as a reading community.

Why Whole-Class Studies Are Important

Throughout the school year, my colleagues and I at the TCRWP find it helpful to divide up the reading curriculum into month-long studies. Much of this work is based on Lucy Calkins' units of study, which are described in the *Art of Teaching Reading* (2001), and Kathy Collins' work, which is described in *Growing Readers* (2004). Hundreds of schools in New York City, as well as schools across the country from California to Connecticut, continue to be supported by the curricular calendars that TCRWP writes each year. Our curricular calendars map out what a year of month-long whole-class studies might look like. Many schools adapt the calendars to meet their own specific needs and align with the available materials. These month-long studies are titled either with the name of a specific genre or one specific habit or behavior of a proficient reader. Regardless of their title, though, each unit teaches a set of reading skills that the genre, habit, or behavior demands. Genre-specific studies may include a study of nonfiction, mystery, historical fiction, poetry, and biography, to name a few. Alternatively, a unit may be titled with a reading habit or behavior such as "Using Print Strategies to Read With Accuracy and Fluency" or "Using Story Elements to Read With Deeper Comprehension."

These whole-class studies offer many opportunities for me to support all the readers in the class. First, they offer exposure to different genres and different purposes for reading across the year. Second, they offer opportunities to expose students to different strategies for deeper reading. Third, they help focus the students and me on working toward just a few goals each month without jumping around in a haphazard way. Fourth, whole-class studies allow different grades to differentiate their curricula so that students are exposed to a variety of whole-class studies as they move from grade to grade, although the same set of reading skills is revisited year after year in these different contexts. For these reasons and probably many more, my whole-class reading instruction is divided up into month-long sections that require students to read books that match the content or genre we are all studying.

At the TCRWP, our whole-class studies focus on many reading skills at a time and spiral throughout the year. This means that students will be using skills such as retelling, making connections, determining importance, and making inferences not only in the fall, but also for the rest of the year. Additionally, the ways in which readers determine importance in narrative realistic fiction stories are quite different than the ways they determine importance in expository nonfiction articles. The whole-class studies support students in being able to work on a skill like determining importance in many genres throughout the year as they progress to more difficult reading levels. The core skills do not change during the year, but the context in which they apply them does.

Prior to beginning a new school year, I sit with grade-level colleagues and map out what kinds of studies the class will be undertaking each month. The year almost always starts with a study of building strong reading habits and behaviors. When mapping out curriculum for the primary grades, I make sure there is a balance of the kinds of books students will be reading and the kinds of studies that support accuracy and fluency as well as comprehension. In the upper elementary grades, most of the units tend to be more comprehension-focused, and I often try to map out a plan that allows for a balance between narrative and non-narrative genres. In either case, once I decide upon the name for the unit, I then decide on what collection of skills that specific genre or habit demands. For example, if I decide my fourth graders and I will embark on a "Mystery" study, I need to also decide what reading skills we will be focusing on inside of this study. Perhaps prediction, visualizing, inference, and synthesis make the most sense.

I work with some teachers who divide their year up into whole-class studies that focus on one reading skill at a time. For example, October may be focused on retelling, and November may be focused on making connections. Our whole-class studies do not follow this structure for a few important reasons. First, strong readers don't just use one skill at a time, so this focus may actually be limiting readers. Second, readers benefit from repeated exposure and instruction around the same skills throughout the year, not just for one month. Third, as readers progress from easier to more difficult reading levels, they need to use these important reading skills in different ways and need support all year long in learning how to use them with more sophistication.

WHY HAVE WHOLE-CLASS STUDIES

- They expose students to different genres and purposes for reading.
- They help students acquire different strategies for deeper reading.
- They focus the class on a few big goals for the month.
- They differentiate the curricula for different grades.
- They support students' use of skills all year long in different contexts.

Examples of Whole-Class Studies

The whole-class studies allow me to set three to five big goals for all the students in a given month and to teach in ways that support their growth towards these goals. Let's imagine it is September, and my whole-class study is focused on building strong reading habits and behaviors. I sit down with other staff developers at the TCRWP as well as teachers and draft a list of student goals to guide the month's teaching. These goals might include: (a) reflecting on the kind of readers they are, (b) choosing books that will support good reading, (c) building routines and structures to support independence, (d) envisioning the world of the story, and (e) retelling the most important parts. Once I have these goals, I generate a list of possible strategies I can teach to help students meet these goals. These strategies will be taught in whole-class instructional time as well as during reading conferences.

The following table shows a list of possible whole-class studies and goals. They are not listed in sequence.

Whole-Class Study	Goals for Readers
Building strong reading habits and behaviors	a. Reflecting on the kind of reader you are b. Choosing books that will support good reading c. Building routines and structures to support independence d. Envisioning the world of the story e. Retelling the most important parts
Character study	a. Identifying the main and supporting characters and their roles b. Inferring character traits and feelings c. Forming interpretations about a character over the entire book d. Making connections about the characters from one book to another book e. Supporting inferences, interpretations, and connections with evidence from the text
Word attack study	a. Using strategies to figure out what new words say b. Using strategies to figure out what new words mean c. Integrating multiple strategies to read for meaning and accuracy
Poetry study	a. Understanding the difference between poetry and prose b. Identifying the tone and reading with expression c. Envisioning the images in poems d. Interpreting poems
Biography study	a. Identifying major events in a person's life b. interpretations about why this person is famous and what kind of person he or she was c. Critiquing the author's point of view d. Comparing and contrasting different books about the same person

Conferring During Whole-Class Studies

Because students will be reading different books at different reading levels, my conferring to support the whole-class study often helps students find the strategies that best match their reading levels and strengths as readers. By using one-on-one conferring time to meet with students, I can teach a whole-class study within a heterogenous class that has readers at a wide range of reading levels. Because all students need to infer the character's traits, for example, but all readers do not infer in the exact same ways, I can support their approximations of inference during conferences. It is possible for all students to meet whole-class goals, but their strategies and levels of sophistication may differ in how they meet these goals.

Most conferences follow a predictable structure—research the reader, decide what to compliment and teach, and then teach the reader. I begin by researching what skills and strategies the reader is already using that align with the current whole-class study, and I make a decision about what to reinforce through a compliment. I also research what skills and strategies I think the reader could benefit from learning and decide what new strategy to teach. In addition, I decide on a teaching method and support the reader's ability to independently use the new strategy.

Researching Within the Whole-Class Study Structure

An important lens to use when researching readers is to figure out how the reader is progressing toward the whole-class study goals. Using the lens of goals that are specific to my current study allows me to differentiate my teaching so that all readers in the class can progress toward these goals at their own level and pace.

Each whole-class goal is usually a reading skill, such as being able to determine the main idea in a nonfiction study. There are many different strategies for determining the main idea of a text depending on the level of the text, the kind of text it is (article, picture book, textbook), and the strengths of the reader. Research allows me to take all of the factors mentioned above into consideration so that I can support the reader with the right strategy for her at this time.

I have found it helpful to carry a whole-class-study overview sheet with me while I confer. This sheet lists the major goals for the study as well as possible strategies to meet those goals. The overview sheet helps me research the reader in ways that quickly help me understand how closely the reader is approximating the goals. Below is an overview sheet for a Content Area study that focuses on reading to learn science concepts. Although the students will be reading science books, the focus of the teaching is on reading skills needed in these kinds of books.

Content–Area Study

- *Readers use their prior knowledge as they learn about a subject:*
  - Before starting a new book think, "What do I already know about this topic?" Then read to see if what you know is in the book.
  - After you finish a section of a book, think, "How did what I just read fit with what I already know about this topic?"
  - Think about what you don't know about a topic and approach a book trying to find new information or answers to questions you have.
- *Readers determine the main ideas about their subject:*
  - Read the title and first paragraph. Think, "What is this section mostly going to teach me about?"
  - Read subheadings and topic sentences and think, "What is this part mostly teaching me about this subject?"
  - Use text features such as diagrams and charts to think about what the section is mostly teaching you.
  - Stop after each page or section and ask, "What is this page or section mostly teaching me about this subject?"
- *Readers use strategies to figure out what a new word says:*
  When you get to a new word you can:
  - look closely at the picture and think about what word would make sense;
  - reread the sentence and think about what word would make sense;
  - use the first few letters to get your mouth ready for the word;
  - look at the first few letters and last few letters (example: Is the word *tree* or *trunk?*);
  - look across the word in chunks. Look at the first few letters, then the middle letters, and finally the ending letters. Then put them together to form a word that makes sense;

  Or

  - find a part of the new word that you already know and use that to figure out the rest of the word (example: If you know *at,* you can figure out *pat.*).

- *Readers use strategies to figure out what a new word means:*
  When you get to a new word you can:
  - look closely at the picture and find clues for what the word means;
  - read the sentences around the word and look for clues for what the word means;
  - try a synonym (word that you think means the same thing) and read the sentence to see if that makes sense;

  Or

  - use text features in the book, such as a caption, word box, or glossary, to find a definition. Then say the definition in your own words.
- *Readers make connections across their books:*
  - As you begin another book about the same topic, begin noticing places that have similar information as the previous book. Mark those places with a Post-it note.
  - As you begin another book about the same topic, begin noticing places that contradict what the previous book taught you. Mark those places with a Post-it.
  - Look across your notes of what you learned and ask yourself, "What is my big idea about all these new things I learned?"
  - Share what you are learning with other readers and ask them, "What is the same or different in your books?" Discuss why different books may teach different things about a topic.

Many teachers use the overview sheet as a resource while they confer. For example, one Thursday morning during the first week of the whole-class content-area study, I observed a second-grade classroom during a staff-development session. I supported Valerie, the teacher, as she approached Sarah. Valerie decided to stand behind Sarah and observe her closely as she read her book. Sarah read each word and when she came to a difficult word she simply skipped it and kept reading. She did read the words on the class's word wall fluently and without much difficulty. Valerie started jotting down her observations in her conferring sheet (Figure 6-1).

Taking the time to observe Sarah for thirty seconds already gave Valerie a lot of information about how Sarah was progressing toward the whole-class

Name: **Sarah**

Date	Compliments I Could Give the Reader	What I Could Teach the Reader
10/16	• recognizing high frequency words from word wall • remembering the pattern in her book	• using strategies to figure out a new word – using clues in picture /words around new word • Knowing that reading always needs to make sense

Figure 6-1.

reading goals. Valerie decided she could have a longer conversation with Sarah about her reading strategies to do more research, but instead she decided to jump in and teach Sarah a strategy for trying to read new words. She couldn't stand to have Sarah skipping over the unfamiliar words and not understand the meaning of her text.

Valerie sat down next to Sarah and complimented her for recognizing the word-wall words and reading them smoothly. Before Valerie decided what to teach Sarah, she glanced at her whole-class study overview sheet to remind herself of the goals for this month. She researched the goal, *readers use strategies to figure out what a new word says.* She could've spent much more time researching each goal, but she had enough information to make a decision about what to compliment Sarah on and what to teach her. She looked over her conferring menu and peeked at Sarah's book. She decided upon a strategy that would help Sarah to read the unfamiliar words based on both what she thought Sarah would be able to handle, and also on what supports the text had. She chose a strategy Sarah would be able to practice right away. She decided to teach Sarah how to use clues in the picture to figure out what a new word might say. Her next conferences could examine the rest of the goals in more depth.

Use Observation as a Research Method

As seen in Sarah's research, observation can yield a lot of information about readers in a short period of time. When I approach a student with clear goals in mind, I can look for evidence of the goals in the student's behaviors, reading logs, and writing about reading. Quickly glancing at the reader and the artifacts of her thinking gives me a focus to start a discussion. When I observe students, I often glance at the goals for the unit and jot down observations for how the goals are or are not being met. I might ask myself such questions as:

- "Which goals are the students approximating?"
- "Which goals are the students ignoring or not attempting?"
- "Which goals do I want to discuss with the student because I can't tell much from observation alone?"

Have Conversations About the Reader's Process as a Research Method

After some quick observing and jotting down of notes, I often begin my conversation by asking about what I did or didn't observe. I might say something like:

- "Can you tell me why you decided to choose this book?"
- "Can you explain how you are using Post-its right now?"
- "Can you show me what you do at challenging parts?"

These questions are genuine in nature and offer the student a chance to explain her process as a reader.

Rather than simply asking the reader to retell or to predict, I typically start by having the reader talk about the reading process she is undertaking before asking her to demonstrate a particular skill. For example, if I see a Post-it note on every page of a book during a whole-class study of characters, I tend not to start by saying, "Tell me who the main character is in your book." This question would let me know if the student can determine the main character, and I may ask that question later, but first I want to find out about the reader's process and why the reader has Post-its on every page. The student's response might let me know what she knows about how to study characters and also give me insight into her reading habits and thought processes.

If the reader says, "I put a Post-it on every part where the main character, Junie, is making a decision and wrote down what that makes me think about the character," then I learn a lot about this reader. The reader's explanation lets me know that he knows who the main character is, that he knows that a character's decisions are important, and that he should slow down and think about the character's motivation at those parts. The student also knows how to record his thinking so he can refer back to it later. Because I ask the reader to discuss his process, I gather much more information about his reading in a shorter amount of time than if I ask a series of smaller questions about each strategy he has been taught or quiz him about the content of the book. I can use the reader's explanation to quickly glance at the goals of the month and determine which strategies he is and is not using.

Listen to the Student Read

While it is important to periodically listen to the reader read aloud, it is just one tool for researching a reader. I listen to the reader if my goal for that month is focused on fluency or word attack strategies, such as figuring out unknown words. I also listen to the reader read aloud if the conversation with the reader makes me think she might be having difficulty reading the words. If I am researching a beginning reader, such as a kindergartener or first grader, I almost always listen to the student read a bit since a lot of the work they do as beginning readers is printwork. If a second-grade reader tells me in our conversation that she is learning about whales in her nonfiction book and that they are fish, this inaccurate statement might lead me to ask the student to read a bit of the book for me, because she might be struggling to read the words too much and the book might be too difficult. Richard Allington (2001) taught me that readers cannot do higher-level thinking and comprehension work if they are struggling to say the words on the page. By listening to a student read, I can quickly tell if the text may be too hard.

If my students are working toward goals in reading with more fluency, I listen to students read in order to assess how they are progressing toward that goal. By fluency, I mean the reader's ability to phrase sentences in meaningful ways, to read the punctuation, to read with intonation and expression, and to read with consistent pacing. When I approach the reader, I prompt the reader to read aloud to me in a way that matches our month's goals. For example, I say, "Can you read to me in a way that sounds like talking?" or "Can you read to me in a way that matches the feeling of the poem?" This prompt allows the reader to show me how she is doing with the goal. I can make teaching decisions based not only on the student's oral reading, but also on my observations and conversation with her.

Sample Research Questions for Fluency	
Fluency Goals for Readers	**Research Questions That Match the Goals**
Reads in meaningful phrases	Can you read to me so that it sounds like talking?
Reads with intonation	Can you read to me so that your voice matches the feeling of the text?
Reads the punctuation	Can you pay close attention to the punctuation and read so that your voice matches it?
Rereads when encounters difficulty	Can you reread any parts that are tricky for you as soon as you figure them out?

Deciding How to Support Whole-Class Study Goals

Sticking to One Big Goal

Once I have researched the reader in terms of how he is progressing toward the whole-class study goals, I decide what to compliment and teach. Sometimes I choose to compliment the use of a strategy that matches one of the big goals and then teach another strategy that goes with the same big goal. For example, I could compliment Kevin for paying attention to a character's decisions and thinking about her motivation. Then I could teach Kevin another strategy for thinking about the character's motivation, such as paying attention to what the character says to others and how she says it. I typically decide to compliment and teach strategies that go with the same big goal when: (a) it is a really important goal, (b) the reader is only using one strategy at a surface level to meet the goal, or (c) the reader is already approximating the strategies and just needs a little more support.

After reading several expository texts with different structures and at different reading levels, I think about what strategies I used to figure out the main idea. In a newspaper article, I noticed I used the title to figure out the main idea as well as the first paragraph because news articles tend to have the most important information at the beginning of the text in case readers don't read the whole article. I noticed that when I read the picture book *Dogs*, by Gail Gibbons, there were no subheadings, so I read a page (both the text and pictures or diagrams) and then stopped and asked myself, "What was this mostly teaching me about?" and kept doing that on each page. After I read many different kinds of expository texts, I listed my strategies on an overview sheet for later use.

Strategy Overview Sheet for One Big Goal

Skill	Strategies
Determining the main idea in expository texts	■ Use the title and first paragraph of a news article ■ Use subheadings and topic sentences ■ Use text features such as diagrams and the accompanying text ■ Stop after each page or section and ask, "What is this page or section mostly teaching me about?"

I use this strategy overview sheet to make decisions about what to compliment and what to teach. If I know I want to support the reader's ability to determine the main idea of an expository text, I will choose one strategy that he is using off this list and compliment it. Then I will choose another strategy off the list *within the same category* to teach the reader. I make my decision based on the kinds of expository texts the reader is reading as well as my knowledge of the reader's strengths.

Too often it can be easy to think of reading skills like a checklist. I am tempted to stop researching and teaching a skill once I notice evidence that the reader is using the skill. There are, however, ways to deepen a skill and get even better at using the skill. For example, I can make homemade bread, but I also can definitely get better at it. My bread is not as tasty, light, or well shaped as my mom's bread. My bread-making skills can definitely be deepened. The same can be said for reading skills. A reader can be able to predict, but she also can be taught ways to deepen her prediction and to do it even better. For this reason, it is important to not view a reading skill as something to be checked off on a list, but instead as something that can grow and be used with greater sophistication. I therefore make my decision based on whether I think the reader can deepen her use of the skill.

Theresa is the kind of reader who uses many strategies, and she's the kind of reader who applies everything I teach her. One Monday morning in the middle of a second-grade nonfiction whole-class study, Theresa was excited to show me what she had been learning about whales. I spent time researching Theresa by observing her behaviors, having a conversation with her, and listening to her read a section of her book. My conferring notes (Figure 6-2) listed what she was already doing and what she could use more support with.

Name: **Theresa**

Date	Compliments I Could Give the Reader	What I Could Teach the Reader
11/14	• making connections across texts – accumulating info about a topic in several books • identifying texts that are too hard for her • using the title to determine the main idea	• using text features – diagrams, charts... • figuring out new vocabulary words • jotting down her thoughts on post-it notes

Figure 6-2.

After looking at my whole-class-study overview sheet, I decided that I wanted to stick to the big goal of determining the main idea because it is so important when reading nonfiction. Theresa was already using a strategy for determining the main idea, and I decided to compliment it: "Theresa, I like the way you are using the headings of your books to help you figure out what they are mostly teaching you about. For example, when you read the heading 'What Whales Eat,' you told me you thought this section was mostly teaching you about the kinds of food whales eat. It is so smart to pay close attention to the headings of articles because they usually do help you figure out the main idea. Please remember to keep doing that all of the time when you read nonfiction. Nice work!" I explained.

I decided to stick to the big skill of determining the main idea and deepening her ability to determine importance. I glanced at the strategy overview sheet that I previously prepared and chose a new strategy off the list to teach Theresa. I decided to teach her to pay more attention to the text features because I noticed she had a diagram in the article I just discussed with her, and she ignored it completely. "Theresa, I want to teach you another important strategy for figuring out what the section is mostly teaching you about. Readers of nonfiction don't just read the heading and words, but also study the text features such as diagrams and charts. These features can also help you figure out what the section is mostly teaching you about." Then I proceeded to demonstrate this strategy for Theresa on my own article and coached her to try it with one of hers. By complimenting and teaching strategies that supported the same big skill from the whole-class study, I helped the reader develop even more sophistication, and helped the reader to expand the context in which she'd use the reading skill.

Supporting More Than One Big Goal

I may also choose to compliment the use of a strategy that focuses on one big goal and decide to teach a strategy that goes with a different big goal. I could decide to support the big goal of being able to have strong conversations about what you are thinking as you read. Then I could choose a strategy, such as preparing for conversations by rereading Post-it notes and deciding which ideas are most important to discuss with a partner. I make this decision when I think the reader is already proficient in a skill and ready to move on to a new skill, when the student is frustrated with one skill and would be better off working on a different skill, or when the student needs help integrating more than one skill.

One Friday afternoon in late October, I approached Julia, a quiet first grader, and watched her whiz through one of her books, barely looking at the words as she recited them perfectly. After talking to Julia about her book and listening to her read two books from her independent reading baggie, I jotted down my research notes as shown in Figure 6-3:

Name: **Julia**

Date	Compliments I Could Give the Reader	What I Could Teach the Reader
10|22	• one to one matching • using the picture and initial letters to read a new word • reading sight words easily • reacting to the text	• choosing books with enough new challenges • looking at the ending letters of new words • slowing down to think about what is happening on every page

Figure 6-3.

I decided to support Julia in two different big goals in our whole-class study on word attack strategies. Prior to beginning the whole-class study, I read Kathy Collins' chapter in *Growing Readers* (2004) and referred to Irene Fountas and Gay Su Pinnell's *Guided Reading* (1996) book to make a strategy overview sheet. The sheet listed strategies for the big goals in the unit, which were: (a) using strategies to figure out what new words say, (b) using strategies to figure out what new words mean, and (c) integrating multiple strategies to read for meaning and accuracy.

I decided to compliment a strategy that supports the third goal of integrating strategies to figure out the words. "Julia I am so proud of you! When you came to a new tricky word, you used the picture to think about what would make sense and you looked at the first few letters to figure out the words. When you got stuck on this word [I pointed to the word] you looked at the picture and saw the boy eating a sandwich for lunch and then you looked at the letter *S* at the beginning and figured out the word was *sandwich*. It is so smart to use both the pictures and the first few letters when you get stuck on a word. Remember to keep doing that from now on," I explained.

After giving the compliment I decided to teach Julia a strategy that supported a different big goal for the whole-class study. I noticed Julia had trouble figuring out what some of the words meant on her page, even though she could say them. I decided to teach a strategy that supported the second goal of using strategies to figure out what a new word means. "Julia, I noticed that you are getting really good at figuring out how to say the new words on the page, but sometimes you don't know what the new word means. Readers make sure they can say the new word *and* they know what it means. I am going to teach you a strategy for figuring out what a new word means. You can look closely at the picture and look for clues. I'll show you what I mean." I proceeded to demonstrate how I looked closely at the picture to figure out what the word *yelped* means by showing her how I noticed the dog was barking at the postman, so maybe *yelped* meant *barked.* Then, I coached Julia to try this strategy from a book in her independent reading baggie. By choosing to support two whole-class study goals in this conference, I helped Julia integrate the different big skills into her reading and not just focus on one skill at a time. I made this decision because I felt Julia was ready to move onto a new skill that went with the one she had previously been working on.

I choose to support more than one big skill when students are: (a) ready to move to a new skill, (b) getting frustrated or not progressing with the same skill over time, or (c) approximating strategies for different skills and are in need of integrating the big skills into their reading lives.

Deciding on a Method of Instruction

When supporting whole-class studies in my conferences, I choose from four main teaching methods—demonstration, example and explanation, shared reading, and coaching—or use a blend of more than one. Each method has its own predictable structures and purposes. I usually make my decisions about which method to choose by thinking about how a reader responded to a method in the past and based on what I know about the way the reader tends to learn best. I also choose a method based on the level of support a reader needs with the particular strategy I set out to teach.

Demonstration Teaching

Lucy Calkins has taught me, and thousands of teachers throughout the country, about using demonstration as a teaching method. Demonstration teaching involves the teacher showing the readers how to use a strategy in a realistic reading setting while thinking aloud about the process and steps. There are four characteristics of demonstration teaching. One characteristic is the teacher does all the thinking aloud for the students and shows them step by step what a proficient reader does while he uses a strategy. Another is the teacher becomes the reader and acts like she is "in the moment" of using the strategy. A third is that the students' job is to watch and notice the steps of the strategy so they have a concrete image to emulate. Finally, it is the teacher's job to clearly articulate what the student should have noticed during the demonstration.

The entire demonstration conference has a highly predictable structure. First, I set the reader up for what he will learn. Then I think aloud and show the strategy step by step. Finally, I restate the strategy in a way that makes it generalizable to all books.

Set the Stage Before the Demonstration Begins

Before beginning the demonstration, it is important to tell students what they will be seeing and what they should be looking for as I show them the strategy. I usually begin by saying something like this: "I am going to teach you how to form an idea about the main character in a book by noticing a character's actions and stopping to think about his motivations. Watch me as I read a little, notice when my character does something, and then stop and ask myself, 'Why is the character doing this?' Pay attention to what I am saying, because I am going to say my thinking out loud for you. My thinking will help you as a reader. Ready?"

I set the reader up to really focus on the important part of my demonstration. If I don't set up the reader and I demonstrate the strategy on *Henry and Mudge* (Rylant 1987), the reader might be noticing how large Mudge is and be thinking about how badly she wants a dog. What I really want the reader to notice is the strategy I use, not the content of my book. I cannot take for granted that a student is noticing what I want her to notice during my demonstrations.

Think Aloud as You Demonstrate Step by Step

After I set the stage for the demonstration, I remember to think aloud while I model. I had to work on this myself. When I first learned to think aloud, it came out more like a *summary* of the strategy. An effective think aloud requires me literally to have a conversation with myself and to be in the moment of the thinking, saying the exact words that come to mind.

For example a *summary* would sound like this:

"I noticed that Henry is asking his parents for a dog. Then I thought that he must be lonely and want a friend."

A *think aloud* would sound more like this:

(I begin reading aloud.) "'Please, Mom and Dad can I have a dog?' Henry asked.' Oh right here Henry is begging his parents for a dog. I wonder why he is doing that? Why does he want a dog so badly? Maybe he wants a dog because he doesn't have any brothers or sisters. He probably wants someone to play with him. I guess he is feeling lonely and wants a companion."

In the summary example, I make the strategy look too easy, as if the idea just popped into my mind. I also do not give student the language and thinking to emulate the strategy. On the other hand, in the think aloud I demonstrate for the student the transition from reading the lines of the book into my thinking. I am not talking to the student. I am talking to myself (or more accurately, thinking to myself and saying it aloud). I also follow the step-by-step strategy I prompt the student to notice in the setup of the demonstration. After watching me demonstrate and think aloud, the student has a clearer picture of the strategy, an idea of what the strategy looks like step by step, and even some language she can emulate by asking herself the same questions I ask myself.

Restate the Strategy the Student Should Notice

After I demonstrate the strategy step by step and think aloud, I often look back at the student and restate what I just did. This has two purposes. The first is in case the student did not "get it" in the setup or demonstration; she has another chance to hear it. Another benefit is to reinforce the language by naming the strategy, so that when I follow up with the student later we have a common language when we talk. I usually say something like, "So I hope you just noticed I read a little, noticed when my character did something, and then stopped to ask myself, 'Why is the character doing this?'" And, I hope, I am greeted with a confirming nod from the student. This summary is a place for me to generalize the strategy so the student not only sees it as something that I can do with my book, but something that can be used with all books. The three parts of the demonstration, therefore, go from a generalizable strategy to a specific example and back to the generalizable strategy. After the demonstration, I begin coaching the reader to try the strategy herself.

CHARACTERISTICS OF DEMONSTRATION TEACHING

- The teacher thinks aloud while showing a strategy to student step by step.
- The teacher becomes a reader and stays "in the moment" while he shows the strategy, thinking aloud when pausing.
- The student observes and notices the steps of the strategy.
- The teacher gives the reader a concrete image of proficient reading.
- After the demonstration, the reader tries out the strategy she just observed.

Example and Explanation Teaching

While demonstration teaching offers students a clear and explicit example of reading strategies, there are times when I choose a less supportive method of teaching—example and explanation. I choose to use explanation teaching when a reader has seen a strategy demonstrated before but still needs more support with it. Example and explanation teaching involves referring back to previous teaching, typically in whole-class experiences such as minilessons, read-alouds, or shared reading. I describe the skill and strategy from a previous whole-class experience but do not actually take on the role of the reader. For example, if I read aloud *Mr. Putter and Tabby Walk the Dog* (Rylant 1994b) and showed a student how I inferred Mr. Putter's feelings, I can refer back to this read-aloud experience as an example of a reading strategy. This is less supportive than demonstration because the student does not see the process step by step in the reading conference; instead I remind the student of the example and explain it.

In the following conference I use example and explanation as a strategy. Just as in the demonstration teaching example above, I am teaching the reader how to infer a character's feelings by using a read-aloud example. Notice how this teaching method differs from the demonstration method above because I don't think aloud and model every step:

> "Remember when we were reading *Mr. Putter and Tabby Walk the Dog* a few days ago? Well, you can all do what we learned from reading that book in read-aloud. We can think about what is happening, look carefully at the character's face in the picture, and pretend we are the character. This can help us think about how the character is feeling. Like when we thought Mr. Putter was worried when we looked at his face in the picture and imagined what it would be like to walk a friend's dog for a week."

Notice how the example and explanation method sounds like a summary of the previous experience with the strategy. It is much more supportive than just stating the strategy though, because I give a concrete example from a recent read-aloud experience. This method is helpful when a reader doesn't need to see a whole demonstration again, but he does need reminding about how the strategy goes.

CHARACTERISTICS OF EXAMPLE AND EXPLANATION TEACHING

- ■ Choose a strategy to teach that has already been taught at another time (usually through demonstration).
- ■ Remind the reader of the example of previous teaching.
- ■ Explain the strategy in a similar way to the original teaching point.
- ■ Ask the reader to try it.

Shared Reading

When I decide that a student needs more support with fluency, I may choose another method of teaching: shared reading. While shared reading is typically a component of balanced literacy that is used in primary-grade classrooms as whole-class teaching, it also can be used within a conference. When I use the shared reading method, I generally begin by choosing a familiar text. Then, I state the teaching point for reading fluently (and I am using *fluency* as an umbrella term for phrasing, intonation, and pacing). Next, I model reading fluently and coach the reader to try it with me. I also help the reader practice in his independent reading book by reading with him and then gradually stopping and just coaching the student to read on his own. In this way, shared reading is a method that requires me to prepare a few texts ahead of time and carry them around with me.

Use a Familiar Text

I carry around copies of a poem or photocopies of a page from a book we have read so that I can use it for shared reading. I make sure the text is familiar so I don't have to work on comprehension with the student, and I make sure the text is on or slightly below the reader's level so he can read the text without much difficulty. I may copy a page of text that has a lot of dialogue from *Poppleton Has Fun* (Rylant 2000), for example, if I have been using the book as my read-aloud. Then I take it out at the beginning of my teaching and remind the student about what's happening in the book and page. I might say something like this:

"Tomas, this is a page from *Poppleton*. It is the page where Poppleton is asking Cherry-Sue if she wants to go to the movies with him. Do you remember that part?"

Another reason why I choose a familiar text is because so much of fluency is dependent on the reader's understanding of the meaning of the passage. In order to read fluently, the reader needs to understand the tone of the passage, who is talking, and the context within which the passage is occurring. Without understanding and comprehension of the text, a reader cannot become truly fluent. For this reason I make sure the student understands the text before working on fluency. I have found that fluency is more than reading in a smooth voice; it also means reading in a voice that conveys the meaning of the passage.

Model Fluent Reading

After I pull out the shared reading text and remind the student about its meaning, I usually start by modeling some fluent reading. This may be a demonstration on the whole text or just a small section of it. I don't just start reading though; I begin by telling the student what I want him to notice about the way I am reading. For example, I might say this: "Tomas, I would like you to listen and pay attention to the way I change my voice when someone is talking to try and sound like the character. In this case, I am going to make my voice sound like Cherry-Sue." Then I proceed to read a section where Cherry-Sue is speaking.

Coach the Reader to Read Fluently

After my demonstration, I want to make sure I give ample time for Tomas to practice reading fluently. I usually begin by having him read the same section I demonstrated along with me to ensure a supportive and successful start. I might say this: "Okay, Tomas, now I want you to try reading that same section with me. Make sure you change your voice when Cherry-Sue is talking. Think about how Cherry-Sue would sound in this part."

I read it with him in unison while I point to the beginning of each line so we can stay together, listening carefully while we read. If I hear him stumble at all, we rewind and try that line again. Once he reads it with success, I ask him to keep reading further in the text without me and coach him along as he reads. Then I coach Tomas to practice reading fluently in his independent reading book as well. The ultimate goal is for students like Tomas to read with fluency independently and at the appropriate level; therefore, at various points I transition a student from practice on a shared reading text to his own self-chosen texts.

Fluency Skills I Can Teach Through Shared Reading Conferences

Reading Punctuation

- Stopping at end marks and making your voice reflect the different types of end marks
- Phrasing according to the commas
- Looking ahead for quotation marks and making your voice reflect the question from the start of the sentence

Reading Dialogue

- Reflecting the character's feelings by noticing the dialogue tags
- Reading in the voice of the character, and having different voices for different characters
- Reflecting the tone of the scene

Phrasing and Intonation

- Reading in meaningful chunks or phrases
- Knowing when to pause for emphasis
- Reading with intonation that matches the tone and action

Rereading

- Going back to reread when you must stop and do a lot of work on a word
- Reading smoothly and not in single-word units

Coaching

Coaching is an important part of every conference when the reader tries out the strategy, but it can also be a method of instruction on its own. Lucy Calkins and colleagues in the *Units of Study* series sometimes refers to coaching as guided practice and uses the terms interchangeably (Calkins et al. 2003; Calkins et al. 2006). Sometimes I decide not to demonstrate or give an example and explanation in a conference. Instead, I begin by having the student start trying the strategy in her book with my guidance and support. The student does all the reading work while I give prompts and tips. I try to make my prompts and tips generalizable to all books so that I am not just supporting the current book.

In the following conference, I chose to simply coach the student. The reader, Henry, was trying the same strategy from the above examples—inferring the character's feelings—but I coached him to try it in his own book. In this example, the *Mr. Putter* book he was reading was one of his own independent reading books.

"What do you think Mr. Putter is feeling right now?" I asked.

"Well, the part I just read said that Mr. Putter was going to walk the dog," Henry said.

"Look at his face and think about what he might be feeling inside," I said.

"Oh, he looks kind of upset," Henry said.

"Now you can also think about how you would feel if you were Mr. Putter," I explained.

"I would be upset, but maybe a little excited, too," Henry stated.

In this brief example of my coaching, I gave Henry prompts to help him infer the character's feelings. I made sure to keep my prompts generalizable to all books. Henry could use this prompt over and over again with all his books by putting in a different character's name.

On another day I had a conference with Tyler, a student who was also reading a *Mr. Putter* book. I decided to support his word attack skills through coaching. While listening to Tyler read during my research, I realized he was getting stuck on words that had suffixes, such as *-ed.* I decided that Tyler needed some strategies for how to figure out words with suffixes.

Tyler had just turned the page in *Mr. Putter and Tabby Pour the Tea.* The page reads, "All day long as Mr. Putter clipped his roses and fed his tulips and watered his trees, Mr. Putter wished for some company." Tyler began reading. "'All day long as Mr. Putter c-cl-,' I don't know that word," he said.

"Look for a chunk at the beginning that you know," I prompted while I covered up the letters *-ped* at the end.

Tyler just looked at the part of the word that says *clip*. "Clip," he said. I then uncovered the ending of the word and said, "Now add the ending." Tyler read, "clip-ed, clipped." He smiled and began reading the next word in the sentence. I prompted, "Go back and read that part to make sure *clipped* makes sense." Tyler nodded because he knew this strategy from some of our previous conferences. He read, "'All day long as Mr. Putter clipped his roses.'" He smiled because that did make sense and then continued his reading.

When he got to the word *watered* he paused and looked up at me. I tried not to look at him because I did not want his strategy to become appealing for help from the teacher. Then I said to him, "Look for a chunk at the beginning that you know." I waited to see if he covered up the ending with his own fingers. He did not, so I picked up his hand and helped him cover the *-ed* part of the word. "Water," he read, and then he moved his fingers and said, "Watered. Oh yeah, that was easy." As I was about to prompt him to reread the sentence and make sure that it made sense, on his own he went back and read, "'All day long as Mr. Putter clipped his roses and fed his tulips and watered his trees.'" He smiled again and continued. "'Mr. Putter,'" he read and then looked closely at the beginning of the word and said, "'wish-ed, wished for some company.'"

At this point I needed to name for Tyler the strategies he used and to remind him to keep using them. So I said, "Tyler what you just did was so smart. When you got to a word that seemed tricky for you, you looked closely at the beginning chunk and covered up the ending. Then you read the chunk and added the ending. In this case the ending was *-ed*. You also went back and reread the sentence to make sure the word you said made sense. These are great strategies to use when you get stuck on a word. Remember to keep doing this from now on as you read."

In this coaching conference I started by heavily supporting Tyler and then gradually supported him less. For example, I initially put my finger over the ending of the words but did not continue doing this every time I coached him. Instead, I moved his hand over the ending and then simply verbally reminded him to look at the beginning then the ending. I did this because I wanted Tyler to be independent by the end of my coaching and not rely on my hand to cover the endings each time.

CHARACTERISTICS OF COACHING

- The reader tries the strategy in his own book.
- The teacher gives tips and prompts to the reader as he tries it.
- The teacher names the strategy for the reader and reminds him to keep using it independently.
- The teacher gradually releases the degree of supports.

Coaching That Supports Independence

It is important that my coaching prompts are not too specific. I want the prompt to be generalizable so that they're something that readers can use over and over again with all books. In Tyler's case I made sure not to say, "Look at the first four letters and think about what people do to roses." That prompt is so specific that it would not help Tyler in the future with other words.

Below are some examples of prompts that are too specific and ones that are generalizable to all reading. Notice that in the column of "too-specific prompts" I often have a question or series of questions, whereas in the "generalizable prompt" category, it is a direct command. Also notice the absence of text-specific or topic-specific words in the "generalizable" prompt category:

If the Reader Is Stuck on ...	A Too-Specific Prompt Is ...	A Generalizable Prompt Is ...
Figuring out the word *skyscraper* even though there is a picture of one on the page	"Look at the building in the picture. Do you know what that really tall building is called?"	"Think about what word would make sense and look at the picture to help you."
Figuring out what the word *distraught* means, although she can say the word	"Well how is he feeling right now after he got caught cheating? Is he sad and upset? Do you think *distraught* could mean *upset?*"	"Read the sentence and think of a word that would make sense there."
Inferring the main idea of an article on dogs	"You said this article was about greyhounds and German shepherds and poodles, so what do you think it was teaching you about? Could it be about different kinds of dogs?"	"Think about what this article was mostly teaching you about."
Figuring out who is talking when the author does not say specifically	"Well, Pinky was talking first and then Amanda was talking back to him. So who could be talking next?"	"Make a picture in your mind of who is talking and say the character's name to yourself after the dialogue."

Sometimes the reason students cannot emulate the strategy I just taught is because I am prompting them in very specific ways. I always want to start with an explicit-yet-generalizable prompt that students can use at both their current point of difficulty and in their future reading challenges when I am not there to support them.

Choosing Methods and Gradually Releasing Supports

I choose my teaching methods based on how much support I think the reader will need. For example, if I am teaching a third strategy for the same skill, I may just need to coach the reader because she is already approximating the skill in a variety of ways. If I am teaching a strategy that was already taught in a previous day's whole-class minilesson, I may give the example from the minilesson and coach the reader because she has already seen a demonstration during the whole-class time. But, if the strategy is new and the student is not attempting the skill independently, I may choose to demonstrate the strategy and then coach the reader to try it in her book. I say *may* because there is no perfect rule for when to use a method. In reality I take into account what I already know about the reader from past conferences and assessments. It may be the case that I've demonstrated a strategy a number of times but the reader still needs a demonstration because she is a visual learner and seeing me do it is more helpful than hearing me talk about it. Knowing my students well and how they respond to different methods influences the methods I choose. While there is no best way to choose a method I do notice there tends to be a spectrum of support. I often use a blend of different teaching methods in a single reading conference. The choice to use a blend of methods is based on constant assessments of how the reader is responding to the current method and whether I think I need to adjust how I'm teaching.

Teaching Methods	When I Would Choose This Method
Demonstration with coaching	When a reader is learning a new strategy or when a strategy has multiple steps or complex parts
Example and explanation with coaching	When a reader has already had a demonstration but needs a reminder of the strategy
Shared reading	When a reader needs support with fluency, phrasing, or intonation
Coaching	When I have taught the strategy but the student is having difficulty applying it to her book, I am helping students integrate a few strategies, or if the strategy is simple and students are already approximating it

Reading conferring requires a series of decisions—what to compliment, what to teach, and what method to use when teaching. Anytime I can make these decisions a little easier, I will. I sit with colleagues and generate strategy menus of possible compliments and teaching points. I practice different teaching methods and think about how different students respond to different methods. All of my decisions are based on my knowledge of each individual reader in the classroom and how I can help each reader meet whole-class study goals in his or her own unique and appropriate way.

Classroom Applications

- Sit with grade-level colleagues and plan out a whole-class study. Read professional books along with your district standards to create a few big goals for the study.
- Create strategy overviews that list the big goals for the study along with a few possible strategies that go with each goal.
- Use the strategy overview sheet to plan for the kinds of conferences you may have this month.
- Look at the overview sheet and ask yourself whether there are strategies that represent each level of reader in your classroom. If not, brainstorm other strategies that match the range of reading levels in your classroom.
- Consider how much support your student needs before deciding on a method of instruction. Keep in mind the reader's history and to what method you think he will best respond.

7

Helping Students Move from Reading Level to Level

"The road to the City of Emeralds is paved with yellow brick."

— THE WIZARD OF OZ, BY L. FRANK BAUM

Marco sat with his head down on the desk, wrapped by his thick fifth-grade arms. The air in the classroom was filled with postrecess, mid-September funk. It was reading workshop, and Marco had just been sent from the meeting area to his reading spot. Students all around him held copies of the books that they had chosen earlier that week from the library and had settled in to read with Post-its and pencils nearby. Marco had no book anywhere in sight.

"I have a special request conference today, " the classroom teacher, Amanda, said to me on a day when I was working as a consultant in her classroom. She led me over to where he was sitting.

"Hi. What's your name?" I started. No response. I tried a few more times to get him to look up, to speak to me, to nod his head, anything. I pulled away from his desk and asked the teacher what was going on. She told me that she just assessed Marco; his independent reading level was M, and he was resisting. He wanted to read a book from the *Animorphs* series he had started, a level T. He was refusing to read at his assessed independent level. I finally got Marco to pick up his head by having a friend, another M-level reader, convince him to read the *Zack Files* series with him because it was really funny, the characters were weird, and maybe they could laugh together. When I talked to Marco later, he told me that he had been at level M since third grade! He said he read all of the books and he was tired of being at that level.

"Marco, I know you want to read the *Animorphs* books," I started.

"Yeah."

"The problem is, I don't want you to use this book for reading workshop. I know your teacher has already talked to you about just-right books, and I know that we both know this is not a just-right book for you."

"Yes it is! I can read it!" Marco protested.

"Marco, reading is way more than just being able to recognize or say most of the words. Reading means being able to follow what's happening, keeping track of all of the characters in the story, and having your own ideas. It's hard to do that when there are many words on every page that are tricky for you," I replied. "Look—"

At this point, I put the *Zack Files* book on the desk in front of him and one book of each level between M and T. I told him that he would need to read a lot of books at each of these levels before he was able to really *read* books from the *Animorphs* series.

"Each of these books represents one of the levels that you need to get strong at reading before you can move to the next level. It's like steps on a staircase. One step at a time and you'll get to your goal. There are going to be hard parts about every book, but I want you to work with me and your teacher to tackle those hard parts one step at a time. Jumping now from *Zack Files* all the way up to *Animorphs* means that there will be so many hard parts for you to handle all at once. I don't want you to feel like reading is frustrating or hard. It should feel fun and comfortable. I love that you're so interested in this *Animorphs* book and you should absolutely keep it. Maybe there's someone at home or a buddy in the class who might be able to read this book with you? I just want to make sure you're reading books more like *Zack Files* for independent reading in school."

He looked at me suspiciously. This was a start.

Reasons for Conferring to Help Students Move to the Next Level

In my role as staff developer, I work in about fifteen to twenty schools each year and meet thousands of readers, many of them reading below grade-level expectations. There are a lot of possible reasons for this—disengaged readers, students with reading disabilities or language delays, or readers who spend time trying to read books that are too hard to read independently. But in cases like Marco's, I often think that the reason some students might be reading below grade level is because they haven't been given instruction in how to move to the next level. So they just stay in one level, month after month, and when it comes time for teachers to assess them, they aren't ready to move to the next level because they still need a skill set that the harder level demands.

When I open a copy of a level-K text (say, *Frog and Toad*) and a level-L text (perhaps *Pinky and Rex*), I notice a huge difference. I see more words per page, less picture support, more dialogue without tags, longer chapters, longer over-all length, many characters introduced on the page, and so on. By looking carefully at what a new level demands of a reader in relation to the previous level from which he came, I see that it's no wonder that students are often challenged by making this step to the next reading level.

I find it to be very effective to use conferring to individualize a reader's needs based on skill and strategy work that a particular level demands. Sometimes, I preteach some content to help a student with prior knowledge in a new book.

In the higher levels (above L), I believe students need to spend a lot of time reading, with strategy instruction as support, not other models of group instruction that introduce the plot. In a series of individualized conferences, I reinforce a set of strategies for a student that the newer level demands. This strategy instruction is more targeted toward resolving potential difficulties when the student reads in this and other books at the new level.

REASONS TO USE CONFERRING TO HELP STUDENTS MOVE TO THE NEXT LEVEL

- Many students need instruction on how to read more a difficult text.
- The strategy instruction that students need is different depending on the strategies the readers are already able to do.
- While many of the skills a reader uses will be the same from one level to the next, the reader will need new strategies and will need to know when to use them in the context of the new level.
- At higher reading levels, students often need strategy instruction or introduction of concepts or time periods rather than book introductions that give away the entire plot.

Researching and Deciding What to Teach

John sat in a bath of sunlight coming through the large windows of his third-grade classroom. Brow furrowed, he held his first real chapter book: *Pinky and Rex and the New Baby*. Until recently, he'd been reading shorter books with chapters that were episodic, where each chapter was a ministory that could be read independently of the rest of the book, not sequentially where the chapters fit together as a whole story. He was excited to be reading at this more advanced level.

"John, how's your reading going today?" I started.

"This book is good," he told me, "because I have a new baby sister, too. I know what it's like to be ignored." I thought about how excited I was to see him making connections between the characters in his book and his own life, and how engaged he seemed in his reading.

As we continued talking about his book, I started to realize he was talking only about the chapter he was currently reading. I knew from studying the characteristics of each level that level L demanded the ability to connect the story across chapters. I had a hunch that John was treating this new level-L book as he had his level-K book: He thought each chapter was its own separate story. Because I knew something about the way the text was formatted at both his new level and the level that he just moved from, I was able to help him with a really important skill of being able to carry information across chapters in his book.

Having a Knowledge of Reading Levels Helps You to Research Wisely

From the beginning of my teaching in a reading workshop, I dutifully looked up titles in the back of Irene Fountas and Gay Su Pinnell's *Guided Reading* (1996) and marked the covers of the books with colored dots, knowing that having these books leveled would help my students to choose books that were just right for them. When assessing readers at the beginning of the year, I took running records and knew that I was looking for a book level that allowed the students to read with fluency, comprehension, and above-ninety-seven-percent accuracy. I fully understood the importance of having levels in my classroom library to allow my students to choose the books they would read quickly and easily, and that having them reading at an appropriate level would help them to better comprehend what they read. And then one day I took a look at the first half of *Guided Reading*. In the front of the book, Fountas and Pinnell identify the unique set of characteristics at each reading level. With this set of characteristics in mind, I was able to level books that weren't listed in the back of the book, and I started to shift my frame of reference to see each of these characteristics as being a skill that students would have to master before they were ready for a new set of challenges in the next level. For example, if I knew that a characteristic of a level-L book is that the chapters are parts of a larger narrative, and that a level-K book often has episodic chapters, or chapters that can be read in isolation without losing meaning of the entire text, then I knew that a reader who was new to a level-L text would need the skill of being able to connect information across chapters. It is true that some skills are repeated from level to level. For example, readers need strategies for tackling new vocabulary in just about every level.

It helps to study levels of texts (either by looking up what other authors have said about this level or by picking up a few different examples at that level) by asking myself, "What might pose a challenge to a reader who is new to this level?" to first determine the characteristics of that level. Next, I ask myself what skill a reader might need in order to tackle that difficulty. Then, I try to identify what questions I would ask and what behaviors I would look for to assess whether the student has a handle on those skills. Finally, I try to brainstorm a list of possible strategies I could teach if I find through my research that the student needs some further work with the skill. I've found it helpful to organize what I've found into a conferring menu so that I can carry it with me as I confer (for more help on developing menus like this, see Chapter 10).

Figure 7-1.

Level L

Research Questions and Prompts	Skill	Strategies
"Tell me how this chapter fits with the ones you've read so far."	Accumulating text (carrying the story from chapter to chapter)	▪ Put a Post-it with a brief summary at the end of each chapter and reread the Post-its when you resume reading the book. ▪ At the start of a new chapter, think about the transition by asking yourself: Who is in this new part? Where are they? Why are they here? How did they get here? ▪ Use your knowledge of story structure—expect a rising action, a problem, a solution to the problem, and a result. Pay attention to where the current chapter fits.
"Show me a word that was new for you. How did you figure out what it meant?"	Figuring out difficult vocabulary	▪ Read the sentence before the hard word, the sentence that contains the hard word, and the sentence after. What would make sense? ▪ Use your knowledge of prefixes, suffixes, and root words (new, unknown words at this level are often polysyllabic).
(turn to a scene with untagged dialogue) "Can you tell me who's talking here and what they're talking about?"	Monitoring for sense (during stretches of untagged dialogue)	▪ Stick in the characters' names (mentally) where there are none to keep track of who is talking. ▪ Envision the two characters and watch them take turns talking. ▪ Use your knowledge of the characters to understand who is talking—ask yourself, "From what I know about the characters, who would most likely be saying this?" ▪ Create voices for each character and read with those voices in mind.
"What ideas do you have about the kind of person this character is?"	Inferring character traits	▪ Notice the way your character interacts with other characters in the scene. Ask yourself, "What kind of person would act that way?" ▪ Think about the character's motivations together with how she is acting in a scene. Ask yourself, "What ideas does it give me about this person?"
"What do you think will happen next?"	Predicting	▪ Notice patterns in a character's behavior to allow you to predict how he will act in the future. ▪ Use what you know about plot (problem, problem worsens, problem gets solved) to predict what will happen next.
"Read a little to me."	Reading fluently in phrases	▪ Sweep your eyes/finger under a few words at a time. ▪ Group .words between punctuation together (commas, quotation marks, periods).
(go to part with dialogue) "Read this part to me."	Reading with intonation	▪ Keep in mind what you know about the character. Read acting like him. ▪ Pay attention to punctuation, and make your voice match the marks on the page. ▪ Lower your voice for narration, and make your voice sound like a character talking when you see quotation marks.
"Did you see any words you didn't know how to read?"	Reading unknown words	▪ Look for prefixes or suffixes that you know. ▪ Think, "Does this look like another word I know?" ▪ Break up the word into manageable parts—syllables.

Researching

When I have a hunch that a student is ready to move to the next level, I decide to do a "research-only" conference. In this kind of conference, I begin by asking all the questions on my conferring menu from that level. I also ask the student to read aloud to me from his or her current book, expecting a very high (near one hundred percent) accuracy rate and fluency and intonation. I also check the student's reading log to see that she has read many books at the current level. If the student is able to demonstrate proficiency in all areas (literal and inferential comprehension, an adequate volume of books has been read, and her reading of the current level is fluent), then I make a plan to see the student in a conference soon to help transition the student to a new level.

RESEARCH TO DETERMINE IF A STUDENT IS READY TO MOVE TO A NEW LEVEL

- The student has read many books on his current level (as indicated on a book log).
- The student can demonstrate mastery of most of the reading skills—including both literal and inferential comprehension—that the current level demands.
- The student is able to read with very high (near one hundred percent) accuracy and with fluency, intonation, and expression in his current level.

I may also decide to do this same kind of research with a student about whom I am concerned because he appears to be "stuck" in a level for longer than I expect. For a student who has been reading a level-L text for a while, I ask such questions as, "How does the chapter you're reading now fit with the chapters that have come before?" because I know that he needs to know how to connect the story across chapters, or "Tell me about the characters in your book" because I want to determine if he is able to keep track of an increased number of characters, and is able to make inferences about who the characters are. I may peek at his Post-its to see if the student is responding to the text in any way that suggests that he is inferring or interpreting, that the student is thinking about a theme or big idea, or that the student is still using his Post-it notes merely to hold onto the information in each chapter. I may watch to see if a reader is using pictures to double-check his comprehension or if the reader is overrelying on them to make sense of the text.

It is also possible that the research I do one day informs a conference that I do another day. I may look across conference notes for a span of time and realize that the student has mastered most or all of the skills that the current level demands, so I then choose to transition the student to the next level.

Methods for Moving Readers to a New Level

Strategy Instruction to Move Readers to a New Level

After researching and determining a student is ready to move to a new level, I may have that student choose a few books at that new level as well as a book or two from the level she is leaving. This student now has what Kathleen Tolan would call a "transitional" collection of books—some from the old level, some from the new. My goal in this conference is to help support a student with one of the demands of this new level. I teach the student one strategy to help with this new skill. Here is one example of how a conference like that might go.

Research and Compliment

"So, Shanique, I can see that you've chosen a few books from the *Judy Moody* series by Megan McDonald in order to try out this new level. And I can also see that you've kept some of your favorite series—*Fox and Friends.* Good. You've got some of each in your baggie. I want to give you a compliment," I said.

"Uh-huh."

"I like how you've chosen a few *Judy Moody* books. That's a really smart thing to do when you're moving to a new level. You know so much already from reading a bunch of books from the same series—these *Fox* books by James Marshall—and now when you get to this new level, you can use what you know from one book in the series to help you with the next book, and the next book, and the next book. It's smart to pick a bunch of books from the same series when you move to a new level."

This is an example of how a compliment can come from just simply noticing something the student is doing or has physical evidence of, such as things that might be written on Post-its, books in the student's book baggie, or trends that you notice from looking at the student's book log. Next, I taught Shanique something by giving a quick example and explanation and supporting her in trying it out.

Teach

I said, "I can't wait for you to get started in this new series because I think you're really going to like these characters—Judy and her little brother Stink! Before you get started, though, I want to give you a little tip about something that might help you to feel like this new level is just right for you. You know how in *Fox and Friends* there are only a few characters you need to keep track of? There's Fox and his little sister, his mother, and a few friends? Well, once you get to this new level, you're going to come across a lot of characters right away. So one of the things that I like to do is to keep track of the characters by jotting a list of their names and something about them on a Post-it or in my notebook, and then I can refer back to it when I get confused."

I pulled out a chapter book that I used often for conferring. It had a bunch of Post-its stuck into it with my own thinking from reading, and tabs that indicate places where I could demonstrate strategies from this book in a conference. I always carried this book with me because it helped me feel ready for just about anything I might encounter in a conference. I showed Shanique how I had a Post-it with my characters' names on it and little reminders like "sister of Russell" and "next-door neighbor" and "tall, skinny teacher." Then I took a moment to explain how this Post-it came to be.

I chose here just to give an example and explanation as my teaching method, although I also may have chosen to read the first chapter of a book and make the Post-it in front of Shanique, thinking aloud to demonstrate how I stop at the end of a page, ask myself if there are any new characters, model rereading to check to make sure I got it all straight, and record my thinking. The method I chose to use is considerably less supportive than demonstration and I chose it for two reasons. One, I knew about Shanique as a reader, and I knew that she was able to understand an explanation of how the strategy was used from past teaching I've done with her. The second reason was that I've already shown the class how to make character Post-its during a read-aloud so it wasn't brand new to her. For students who are struggling and need the opportunity to see me work through the difficulty with the strategy, I would choose demonstration over this method. For strategies that have not been previously taught in minilessons, prior conferences, or read-alouds, I also recommend demonstration. I began by explaining the strategy to her:

"So, as I was reading, I wrote down the characters' name as I first saw it and then I read on asking myself, 'How is this character related to the main character? What can I write down on my Post-it to make sure I remember who she is?' and then I wrote it down. Do you see that?"

"Yeah. I see you put the characters' names. You have a lot of characters in your book! Here you put down something about them, like how they look or who they are related to," she said.

"You've got it. Why don't you try this out? Read the first few pages of your book and take this Post-it to jot down the names of who you meet. Remember to ask yourself, 'How is this character related to the main character, and what can I write down so I can remember who this person is?'"

As Shanique set off in her book, I opened up my conferring notes to Shanique's section and recorded what I just did. I jotted down that I taught her a strategy for holding onto the many characters she's going to meet in her new book. I made a note that I wanted to check in with her soon to make sure she was connecting one chapter to the next as well. I peeked at her book log and noticed that she had read a few books from the *M&M* series, which are longer level-K books, so I thought she might have had some experience with this important strategy of connecting the chapters that she will need in level-L books. By now, she'd had a few minutes to try the strategy of writing down character names to help her remember, so I peeked over her shoulder and saw that she'd written "Stink = Judy's brother. He's annoying to her. She wants him to leave her alone."

"Shanique—good job identifying a new character. Take a peek at mine again. What do you notice that's different between yours and mine?"

"Uh, you didn't write as much as me."

"Yeah. For the purpose of this strategy, you don't need to retell the scene. Just jot something to help you remember who the character is in relation to the other characters. What, of all you've written, do you think you need to help you to do that?"

"Um, just that Stink is Judy's brother," she said.

"Okay. You don't have to erase this, but for the next character, just jot down a quick note, okay?"

She continued and jotted down, "Rocky—Judy's best friend."

I reinforced the teaching point again and sent her back to read independently for a while. "Nice, Shanique. Keep up the good work of jotting down just the characters' names and a quick reminder of how they are related to the main character, or a note to help you remember who they are. I'll check back in with you soon to see how this book is working out for you!"

Book Introductions to Move Students to a New Level

Using book introductions as a method is unique to conferences for the purpose of moving students to a new level. Sometimes I feel that a student needs more than just a single strategy to help to transition her from one level to the next. This may be because the text that the reader has chosen has something unique about it in addition to being a new level. One example of this is if a student is moving from level K to L and has chosen the *Amelia Bedelia* series by Peggy Parish. This is a series that not only is challenging to a new level-L reader because of text density, vocabulary, and untagged dialogue—features typical of level L—but it also demands that readers know idioms. In a book introduction, I may decide to introduce the text so that the student understands the idioms, because without that understanding the whole fun of the book is lost.

Another example where I might want to give a book introduction is when the student has chosen to read a text that is set in a historical time period. In a higher-level book like level-T's *Bud, Not Buddy,* by Christopher Paul Curtis, for example, the student needs to have some knowledge of the foster-care system, America in the 1930s, and the Great Depression. In introducing this book, I'd want to highlight a few key vocabulary words and concepts that would help the reader to understand and enjoy the book.

Of course, choosing this method of teaching in a conference requires that I know enough about the book to get the reader started. For this reason, it's helpful to plan out the conference more than I normally would. I use Fountas and Pinnell's guide in *Guided Reading* for a good book introduction to help me with this (Fountas and Pinnell 1996). I try to give away key elements of the plot, use the characters' names in the introduction, or perhaps point to pictures (if there are any) to give a visual of what I'm saying while I'm introducing the text and to highlight key vocabulary words and concepts. In this kind of a conference, the teacher does a lot of the talking. This conference definitely requires a follow-up soon after the initial one because I send the reader off to be independent after I introduce the text and coach slightly on only a small part.

The book-introduction conference may start by engaging the student in wanting to read the book. I might ask a question asking her to relate the main theme of the plot to her own life. If, for example, the character is jealous about a new baby sister on the way, I might ask the reader to remember a time when she's been jealous.

Then, I summarize the plot. When I summarize the plot, I often give most of it away. Depending on the student, I turn the pages of the book as I talk about the story, pointing to pictures that are relevant and might help the student if she gets stuck along the way.

Next, I make sure to highlight particular things that might pose difficulty for the student. I keep in mind the reader might not have prior knowledge about a unique aspect of the text, such as time periods, difficult text features, or content. Here, my teaching method is to introduce the reader to what she'll encounter in the text through explanation or even through showing photographs or relating it to an experience she has had.

Balancing Instruction Focused on Levels and Instruction Toward Unit Goals

It is crucial that this chapter is not misunderstood as a promotion of teaching skills only pertaining to reading level. It's important that students have access to a rigorous whole-class curriculum through minilessons and read-alouds, and that my conferring not only supports my students in their levels, but also supports their thinking about the unit on which our class is focused.

Classroom Applications

- Study the levels of the books in your classroom. Having a sense of the characteristics of a reading level makes it a lot easier to confer when you aren't familiar with the text.

- Know difficulties to introduce to help to make a student's transition to the next level smoother.

- Transfer your knowledge of reading levels to a conferring menu. This will help you to have planned out the research questions to assess for particular skills, and will provide you with a menu of possibilities for strategies to teach if you notice they're not showing evidence of a skill.

- Think about the method of instruction that makes the most sense to help a student move to a new level. If what the reader most needs is instruction around a strategy, consider a research-decide-teach conference. If there is a book that poses some particular challenge that's unique to the book—for example, it's written about a time period that the reader doesn't have knowledge of—you might consider using a method borrowed from guided reading and plan to introduce the text.

Holding Students Accountable for Previous Teaching

"'Moo are you thinking again?'
'A small think,' said Moo."

— MINNIE AND MOO GO DANCING, BY DENYS CAZET

I have been an aspiring guitar player for some time. It started as an interest, but after purchasing my own guitar I began taking lessons. My guitar teacher met me once a week at my apartment for one hour. In those one-hour sessions I noticed that he usually focused on one song for a few sessions. He would teach me the necessary chords for the new song on day one and then follow up during the next few sessions. He'd teach me one way to make the chord in session one and in the follow-up sessions he would assess how I was doing with the song (and most importantly the new chords). I think he was assessing whether I could handle a new, more difficult way to play the chord, whether I needed more practice with the current way of making the chord, or whether I was struggling so much that he had better teach me the simplest way possible. Sometimes he simply decided to "graduate" me to a new song and forego more teaching around the previous song. What I now realize about the assessments my guitar teacher made was how important the follow-up to previous teaching was for both my engagement in learning to play and also for my continual improvement as a guitar player.

Too often when I teach something new, both the student and I grow overwhelmed by the amount of new learning that is required. It can be tempting to begin teaching a new skill each time I meet with the learner to try and give her as much information as possible as quickly as possible. But I have found that rushing through many new skills is rarely what is best for the student. In many cases it is helpful to stick with one skill for a while before moving on to a new skill in order to keep the student engaged in the learning process and to help her perform some skills well. Often, less is more.

Why Follow Up on a Previously Taught Skill

There are many reasons why starting a reading conference by following up from previous teaching is beneficial to students. First, by sticking with one skill for a few conferences I am holding the reader accountable to implement what I taught her. It can be tempting for young readers to only practice what I teach them on the day I teach it, never to think about it again. By following up with skills and strategies I previously taught, I am sending the message to students that once they are taught a new skill and strategy the expectation is that they incorporate it into their reading lives from now on. Second, when I follow up on a previously taught skill I can lift the level of sophistication by which a student can implement the skill. I can teach more challenging strategies while still working toward the same skill. This allows students to move at their own pace toward more challenges and often fosters greater success because of the incremental nature of building up toward difficult strategies. Third, by sticking with previously taught skills over time I offer students multiple supported attempts at approximating the skill and strategy. Many students benefit from repeated exposures and opportunities to practice the skill with my support. Another reason is that by following up on previously taught skills I can prepare and plan for my next conferences. If I know I am continuing my work with a student around a particular skill, I gather helpful materials ahead of time or reference resources to think more deeply about what strategies would help the reader with the skill. In addition, I can teach students how to integrate multiple strategies from past teaching to use in unison. Finally, by following up with previously taught skills I can reflect on my own teaching practices. Assessing whether or not my students are able to approximate what

I previously taught them gives me the chance to assess whether I am teaching in ways that "stick"—by that, I mean whether what I teach today is something the student is able to do continually after I am gone. If not, I can reflect on my own teaching decisions and practices and adjust them accordingly.

WHY IT IS IMPORTANT TO FOLLOW UP ON PREVIOUSLY TAUGHT SKILLS

- It holds students accountable for past teaching.
- It supports students' growth toward greater sophistication within one skill.
- It offers students multiple opportunities for practice with my support.
- It helps me to prepare for my next conferences.
- It helps me teach readers to integrate multiple strategies from previous teaching.
- It offers me opportunities to reflect on my teaching decisions and practices.

Researching in Ways That Assess Previously Taught Skills

When I approach students for a follow-up conference, I typically begin by rereading my past conference notes about the reader quickly. I reread them thinking about what past skill I taught and how I can assess how the reader is progressing with the skill. I also think about how well the reader is able to combine strategies she already knows how to do.

One of my third-grade readers, Amanda, was in the beginning of a unit of study that focused on getting ideas about characters. It was early October, and Amanda was reading several level-M books. She began the year reading several level-K and -L books, such as *Pinky and Rex* books and *Horrible Harry* books. She was the kind of reader who enjoyed books written in a series. She liked to study characters in books even before our class started this formal study of characters. During the first week of this whole-class unit of study on characters, I already had conferred with Amanda, and my conferring notes are shown in Figure 8-1.

Name: _Amanda_

Date	Compliments I Could Give the Reader	What I Could Teach the Reader
10/6	• Keeping track of main character • jotting notes about character on post-it notes • inferring the character's feelings	• having a purpose for her post-it notes • inferring the character's traits - noticing how the character interacts with others

Figure 8-1.

As I approached Amanda for the second time during the whole-class unit of study on characters, I wanted to make sure I was following up with my previous teaching. I read my notes for what I taught Amanda previously, which was how to infer the character's traits. I found this information by looking at the right-hand column of my notes and by noticing which bullet had the teaching point

Figure 8-2.

written next to it with the date I taught it. It was helpful for me to have written both the previous skill (inferring character traits) and the strategy I taught (to notice how the character interacts with other characters and then ask yourself, "What kind of a person would do that?"). I knew that when I approached Amanda for the conference, I could begin by asking her about how the new strategy was going.

I began the conference by sitting beside Amanda and researching to follow up with the last conference's teaching point. I began with the following:

"Last time we met, you were doing a good job of having ideas about the way the characters are feeling in different parts of the story. I taught you about how you can have ideas about the character's traits—a word that describes the kind of person that character is. I was wondering if you could show me some places where you have tried to have ideas about the character's traits."

SOME COMMON FOLLOW-UP RESEARCH QUESTIONS

- Can you show me some places where you (last teaching point)?
- How is (last teaching point) going?
- What has been tricky for you with (last teaching point)?

The research phase of follow-up conferences is often more focused, and perhaps shorter, because I am researching for two things: first, how well the student is able to show evidence of trying the one particular skill that I'm following up on, and second, how well the student is integrating that one skill with other unit goals. I also can research quickly because I make decisions about what kind of research to do. When I am starting my research in an open-ended way, I usually observe the reader, talk with the reader, listen to the reader read, and look at a reader's writing about reading from her Post-its or quick jots in the reading notebook. But in a follow-up conference, I won't necessarily need to do all these forms of research. Instead, I generally use the research method that best matches the previously taught skill or integration of skills. If I am researching the student's fluency or reading rate, I begin my research by asking the student to read a little bit to me. I might even take a running record of the oral reading in order to have an assessment I can refer back to. While listening to the student read I am using the lens of what I taught her last time. For example, if I previously taught the student to work on fluency by taking a short breath at the end of punctuation marks, such as periods, I will ask the student to read aloud a section of the book while I listen for evidence of her pausing at the end marks. Of course I will notice many other needed strategies when I listen to her read, but my main focus will be on taking the breath at end marks because that was the previously taught strategy. I record any new observations in my records for later use.

If I am researching the student's word attack strategies, I begin by asking the student to read a bit aloud to me, and I possibly take a running record. Again, even though this research might help me notice several possible strategies to teach the student, I will mainly focus on what I previously taught her. For example, if I taught the reader how to look across a tricky word in chunks from left to right, I listen and observe her reading with a focus on what she does when she encounters tricky words. If the reader is someone who is able to describe her own reading process, I also could begin my research by saying, "Could you please show me a place where you found a tricky word and show me what you did to figure it out?" Both listening to a student read and asking her to show me a specific place where she used a previous word attack strategy allow me to start my research in ways that follow up with previous teaching.

If I am researching the student's comprehension, I start by having a conversation with her about her book. I begin by asking questions that follow up with the previously taught strategy. Amanda's conference is an example of a comprehension follow-up conference. Another example is if I previously taught the reader how to retell important events sequentially. I start this follow-up conference by asking the reader, "Can you tell me the important events from your book in the order they happened?" Or, if I taught this reader to mark the important events in the book with a Post-it note that has a star on it, I could start my research in this way: "Can you use the Post-its with the stars on them to tell me about the important events in your book? Start from the beginning." While this sort of comprehension work is literal, I would follow up with more inferential skills if I notice the reader understands the text on a literal level. I want to make sure my comprehension teaching pushes readers toward higher-level thinking skills.

If I am researching the student's reading behaviors and habits, I start by observing the student. Because students, like adults, usually will change their behavior when they know they are being watched, I try to stand back a little bit while observing them. Of course, I also work hard to establish a classroom culture where students are not only accustomed to being watched as they read, but one in which students proudly show off their strategies. If I previously taught the reader how he can stay focused on his reading by turning his body away from the table and keeping his eyes and mind on the book, I can observe how this strategy is or is not working. I look to see if he is turning his body away from the table and if his eyes and mind appear to be focused on the book. I also may choose to have a brief conversation with the reader to do some further research about how the new habit is going. I begin by saying, "How is the new reading habit going? Is it helping you to turn your body away from the table?" Taking just thirty seconds to observe the reader and another thirty seconds to ask him about the new habit helps me assess how the previously taught habit is going and whether we should establish it as part of the student's new daily routine.

While I always have one eye toward looking for evidence of a particular skill that I recently taught, I want to also always make sure that the student is also integrating that one skill with others. I never want to send the message that a reader only uses one skill at a time. To research this, I look to see whether the reader knows how to use a repertoire of strategies that I taught in whole-class studies, previous conferences, and even in previous months of the year. In this way, I hold students accountable for all the teaching I have done and not just this month's or this week's. If I find the reader is not integrating strategies, I might choose to teach her how to integrate the strategies she already knows rather than teach a brand-new strategy.

The following is a list of research methods that match different kinds of skills.

If the Previously Taught Skill Was a Goal Linked to . . .	I Will Start My Research By . . .
▓ Fluency or reading rate	▓ Listening to the student read and possibly taking a running record
▓ Word attack strategies	▓ Listening to the student read and possibly taking a running record
▓ Comprehension	▓ Having a conversation about the book and quickly looking at the writing about reading
▓ Reading behaviors and habits	▓ Observing the student and having a conversation
▓ Integration of strategies	▓ Observing and/or listening to the student read

Deciding How to Follow Up

Once I feel I have done enough research in order to figure out how the reader is doing with the previously taught skill and strategy, I have some decisions to make. The decisions are made quickly but, in fact, are usually the most difficult part of the conference for me. I decide if the student is ready to move onto a new strategy for the same skill, if the student is ready to work on a new skill altogether, or if the student needs practice integrating one strategy that he's learned recently with the other strategies from the unit of study. Often, this decision is based on how closely the reader is approximating the skill independently. I'll use my conference with Amanda as an example.

After researching Amanda's use of noticing the character's interactions with others to infer her traits, I made my decision. Amanda told me the following:

"Well, when I was reading *Junie B. Jones and the Stupid Smelly Bus*, I noticed a pattern. Junie is kind of a show-off when she is with her teacher Mrs. Like when she first met Mrs., and Junie told her she knew all the letters of the alphabet but she didn't feel like telling them right now, or when Junie told Mrs. she could print her name beautifully and didn't need any help. This made me think that Junie B. is the kind of character who wants her teacher to think she is smart and doesn't need any help," Amanda explained.

I quickly glanced at Amanda's book and read a few of her Post-it notes. She had three Post-its with the word "show-off" written on them. I read the text under each Post-it and realized that Amanda was able to infer the character traits by noticing the character's interactions with others.

I had to decide if Amanda would benefit from another strategy for inferring the character's traits or if I should move on to another reading skill. In this case I decided to teach Amanda a further strategy for inferring character traits. I made this decision because Amanda was in the early stages of a whole-class study focusing on characters and because I did not see any other evidence in her Post-its or talk that she knew another strategy for inferring character traits. Amanda was able to learn the past strategy fairly easily, and I was confident she could handle a few more strategies for inferring. The new, more sophisticated strategy I chose to teach could be how to put together ideas into a bigger idea, how to use ideas to make predictions, or how to use the idea in one book to get ideas about the characters in other books.

After I made the decision that Amanda was able to independently apply the inferring strategy, I noted it on my conference notes. I also took the opportunity to compliment Amanda on her use of the strategy to infer the character's traits by noticing her interactions with others (see Figure 8-3).

"Amanda, I am so proud of you! You are the kind of reader who gets ideas about the character by noticing the way she interacts with the other characters in the book. You did this when you said Junie B. was the kind of character who wants her teacher to think she is smart and you think she is a show-off. I want you to keep paying attention to a character's interactions

Name: __Amanda__

Date	Compliments I Could Give the Reader	What I Could Teach the Reader
10/6	• Keeping track of main character • jotting notes about character on post-it notes • inferring the character's feelings	• having a purpose for her post-it notes • inferring the character's traits - noticing how the character interacts with others
10/10	• inferring the character's traits - says." Junie B. is a show-off."...	• getting more than 1 idea about the character

Figure 8-3.

so you can get ideas whenever you read books with characters. Great work!" I wrote the compliment—infer the character's traits—in my conferring notes.

Imagine Amanda was not able to infer a character trait, but said she was able to find a place where the character had an interaction. I might have taught a different strategy for inferring character traits, such as paying close attention to the places where the character is talking and then thinking about what kind of a person would talk like that.

Instead of teaching Amanda a new strategy for inferring character traits I could have taught her a new skill, such as reading with intonation that matches the character's feelings. I would teach her a strategy for reading with intonation such as thinking about how a character is feeling and making her voice match the feeling—reading in a happy voice, a scared voice, an anxious voice, and so forth.

Creating a list of different reading skills with at least two strategies per skill helps me to make decisions. This chart helps me to remember different strategies that go with a skill.

Skill	Strategies
▪ Retelling to monitor for understanding	▪ Touch each page of your book and tell what happened. ▪ Tell the main things that happened to the character. Tell it across your fingers by touching one finger and then the next to be sure you tell them in order.
▪ Inferring about the characters	▪ Notice when a character does something and ask yourself, "Why did he do that?" ▪ Look for patterns for how the character deals with conflict and think about why she does that.
▪ Reading with intonation	▪ Notice the punctuation on the page and make sure your voice matches it. ▪ Use the ideas you have about the character's feelings and read in a way that reflects those feelings.

Deciding on a Method of Instruction

My methods for instruction in a follow-up conference depend on the level of support I think the reader needs. In fact, the reason the reader may have struggled with the previously taught strategy may have been that I did not offer the reader enough support in the previous conference or I may have offered too much support without taking the time to assess the reader's strategies. There are particular methods of instruction I tend to use. I choose the method—either demonstration, example and explanation, or coaching—depending on what I notice while researching the reader.

Below are three examples of how I could teach Amanda the same strategy but in different ways, depending on the method of instruction. In all three examples I teach Amanda to use her ideas about the character to predict what the character may do next.

Demonstration

If I decide to teach Amanda the new strategy using demonstration, then I show her the strategy step by step as I say my thinking aloud. I begin the demonstration by setting Amanda up for what to notice. The demonstration might sound like this:

"Amanda, I think you are ready to use your ideas about the character to predict what she might do next. Watch me as I show you how I use my idea about the character to predict what he might do next with my book.

"Remember how I started reading *The Stories Julian Tells*? Well, I have an idea about Julian. I think he is the kind of character who worries a lot that his dad will be mad at him. Like in the first story, when he and his little brother snuck into the kitchen and ate the pudding his dad made for his mom. He wasn't supposed to eat the pudding and, once he realized he ate too much, he decided to hide. He didn't want to get in trouble with his dad. Julian always seems to worry about his dad catching him doing the wrong thing, but he keeps doing the wrong thing anyway."

In the previous section I made sure to use a familiar book to Amanda so she could focus on my strategy and not the content of the book. I then continued:

"I have a few Post-its in this book with my ideas about Julian and wrote the word 'sneaky' on a few of them. Julian is sneaky because he misbehaves and tries not to get caught. Because I already know this about Julian, I am wondering what he might do in the next story. Well, the next story starts off with Julian and his little brother looking at gardening catalogs. I am not exactly sure what Julian will do next, but I do think he will do something wrong and try to hide it from his dad. Maybe he will accidentally spill something all over the catalog and then hide it from his dad so he won't get in trouble. That would be a sneaky thing to do."

In this example I showed Amanda step by step how I used a strategy she already knew—inferring character traits based on how the character interacts with others—to predict what the character might do next. Because I chose to use demonstration, I used a familiar book to Amanda (a former read-aloud text) and showed her my thinking as I used the strategy. After this demonstration, I coached Amanda to try the same strategy in her own book.

Example and Explanation

If I decided to teach Amanda the new strategy using example and explanation, then I would remind her of the strategy from previous teaching I did during the read-aloud. I would pull out the read-aloud book that I carry with me when I confer. I would use a familiar book because it makes referring back to the example of the strategy much easier. The example and explanation might sound like this:

"Amanda, do you remember when we read *The Stories Julian Tells* and we talked about our ideas about Julian?"

Amanda nodded her head and I showed her the book to make sure she really remembered. "When we were reading that book we all shared ideas about Julian, and I remember one of those ideas was that Julian is sneaky; he often misbehaves and then tries to hide it from his dad so he won't get caught."

Amanda nodded her head and smiled, showing me she recalled our ideas about Julian. I pointed to a class chart we made with our ideas about Julian jotted down, and then I continued: "Well, I hope you also remember how we used our ideas about Julian to predict what he would do next. Remember, we thought Julian was going to spill something all over the catalog and then hide it. In the first story we noticed Julian tends to be sneaky, and we used that idea to think about what he might do in the next story. You can do the same thing in your book. You can use an idea you have about the character to predict what he will do next." I made sure to use language similar to the language we used when we originally discussed this strategy during the read-aloud.

Next, I began coaching Amanda to try the strategy in her own book. Because this is an example and explanation conference, I didn't show her the strategy step by step; instead I referenced previous teaching from the read-aloud and reminded her of the strategy with an explanation and visuals. I only choose to use the example and explanation method if I have already taught this strategy at some other point, typically during the read-aloud or minilesson.

Coaching

If I decideed to coach Amanda to try the strategy as the sole method of instruction, I would have started by stating the strategy and then continuing to help her try it. It might have gone like this:

"Amanda, I think you are ready for a new strategy. Today I want you to try to use the ideas you already have about the character in your book to predict what she might do next. Can you find a Post-it with an idea you have about Junie so far?" I stated the strategy and then got her started.

Amanda fliped through her Post-it notes and went back to the notes she wrote that said Junie is a troublemaker. "One of my ideas about Junie is that she is a troublemaker," she said.

"Great! Now I want you to read a little bit of the next chapter and tell me what you think Junie might do next based on your idea that she is a trouble-maker." I broke the strategy down for her into parts. First I helped her find the place where she had an idea, and then I coached her to read on and make a prediction.

Amanda read the first few paragraphs and said, "Junie is going to get in a fight on the bus."

"Why do you think that?" I asked. I wanted to make sure she was basing her prediction on the idea she formed.

"Because Junie gets mad easily and yells at kids and causes trouble a lot," she explained to me. Depending on how much coaching a reader needs during the first attempt at a strategy, I may stick around a little longer and coach her to try it a second time with a little less supportive coaching.

"Amanda, you did a nice job of thinking about an idea you had about Junie to predict what she might do next. Now you can read and see if she does get in a fight . . . or does something else to get herself in trouble. Remember to keep doing this all the time; use your ideas about the character to predict what she might do next." I checked back in with Amanda later in order to see if she confirmed her prediction as she read further or if she revised her thinking.

In this coaching conference, I did not demonstrate or give an example—I just helped Amanda try the strategy herself. I tried to ask her questions that would help her with all books and not just this one. For example, I said, "What makes you think that?" This is a good question to think about in all books. My coaching set Amanda up to have success in this book and also in the future.

Choosing a Method

There is no "wrong" method of instruction in a reading conference, but it helps to decide how much support you think the reader will need with the strategy. If I am teaching something new or really sophisticated, I tend to demonstrate the strategy and then coach the reader to try it. Another reason I choose demonstration is if the reader is really struggling with a strategy and I think showing her my process again would help. On the other hand, if I already have done some recent teaching during the mini-lesson, read-aloud or shared reading times, I may choose not to demonstrate and instead to refer back to the example and explain it again to the reader. This method is effective when the previous teaching was done recently and was memorable, as read-alouds often are. There are also times when I choose to coach the reader because I think she needs a little support to transfer what's been taught into her own reading, so a demonstration or example is not necessary. I also choose coaching as the sole means of instruction when the strategy I am teaching is the kind that readers use over and over again, such as reading punctuation marks. Coaching is supportive for strategies that need to be practiced again and again. I also find that I use coaching often when I am teaching students to utilize a repertoire of strategies, not just one strategy at a time. Often, being the voice in a student's ear as as he reads supports him to not just think about the character, but also make sure he's sweeping his eyes under the word, and stopping at the end of a chapter to go back over the most important events. By coaching a student to integrate multiple strategies while in the act of reading, it often helps to give him the "feel" of reading proficiently.

It is important that I follow up with previous teaching so readers have multiple attempts with support to become independent in a skill. It is also important for me to hold students accountable for what I have already taught

Method of Instruction	Why I Would Choose This
■ Demonstration	■ This is a new skill. ■ This is a more sophisticated strategy. ■ This is a simpler strategy and the reader really struggled with the previous one.
■ Example and explain	■ This is a more sophisticated strategy, but I exposed it to the reader in read-aloud shared reading, or a mini-lession.
■ Coaching only	■ This is the same skill, but the reader needs help with independent application. ■ This is a strategy the reader will need to use over and over again. ■ The student needs practice integrating many strategies.

them. It is too common that students use a strategy for a day or two after they have a conference and then rarely use it again. By following up on my previous teaching, I help readers continually use strategies until they become a natural part of their reading process.

Classroom Applications

■ Start taking notes while you confer. Write down what you teach the reader. After a few conferences, look to see if you tend to bounce around from skill to skill or whether you stick with one skill over a few conferences.

■ Sit with colleagues and create lists of several strategies for the big skills you are teaching. Use the list as a menu of possible strategies to teach in conferences.

■ Practice rereading your conference notes and then beginning your conferences by asking readers to show evidence of how they tried the last strategy you taught them.

■ Jot down the method of instruction you use in your conferring notes. Then look for patterns. Do you always coach? Do you always demonstrate? Push yourself to try new methods of teaching.

■ Carry a read-aloud book with you while you confer so you can refer back to it in an example and explanation or demonstration conference.

9 Improving Student Conversations About Books

"Mr. Putter read and read while Tabby purred and Zeke wagged."

— MR. PUTTER AND TABBY CATCH THE COLD, BY CYNTHIA RYLANT

On Friday afternoon, I finished my third individual conference for the day. I glanced around the classroom and saw readers in corners cuddled up with books and Post-it notes, and readers sitting at desks with books held up to their noses, smiling. Someone across the room let out an "I knew it!" and quickly marked the page with a Post-it. We were a week into our whole-class study on reading mysteries in same-book partnerships.

"Readers, eyes up please." I waited a moment as the students slowly blinked their eyes away from their story worlds and back to the reality of the classroom. "Readers, we're going to start partnership time now. You all have a collection of Post-its in your books where you've jotted some thinking today as you were reading. Take a peek at what you've written and decide on the one or two that you really feel are worth talking about." I circulated for a minute while the students looked over what they'd written, pulling one or two notes out of their books. "It looks like everyone's got an idea in their hands. Go ahead and turn to your partner and start talking."

I walked over to one partnership and listened in. Steven started to tell his partner, Theresa, all about the clues he was gathering in his mystery book, *Cam Jansen and the Mystery of the UFO* by David Adler. "Well, here it says that most UFOs end up being something like airplanes or weather balloons, so maybe it's going to turn out that it's no big deal after all," he began.

"Determining importance," I thought. "Predicting."

His partner, Theresa, challenged him, "Yeah, but later it says there were many lights that moved apart. Planes don't do that, so that doesn't go with what you think. I think it is a UFO! I saw a show on UFOs once on TV, and there was this cluster of lights and then they all separated."

"Critiquing ideas," I thought. "Predicting. Activating prior knowledge."

I was seeing evidence of the skills I taught Steven and Theresa and felt as though I had a glimpse into their brains when I listened to them talk. Conferring into partnerships allows me to use students' talk as an assessment opportunity, as if I have a window into what they're thinking about their books.

Why Confer During Talk Time

Most classrooms in New York City have either partner reading or partner talk built into the weekly reading-workshop time. The youngest readers sit side by side with a book in the middle of their laps and carefully read each page to each other, stopping to smile, frown, or giggle at parts that make them have strong reaction. Older readers sit facing each other with passages in their books marked as they have conversations about the books they are reading and what they are thinking about their books. In the second half of the school year, many upper-grade readers spend time two or three times a week in book clubs where four or five students read the same book and meet with marked passages and questions to discuss with the other members of their group. Each of these structures offers teachers a natural venue for conferring into conversations.

Conferring during partner talk and clubs allows me to glimpse inside a reader's brain, to see the invisible brainwork she is attempting. When a reader talks about her books, she is giving me a sense of how she is constructing the meaning of the text. When a reader tells her partner that a character in a book is not very smart because he keeps getting into trouble, I gain insight into that reader's thinking. When the student's reading partner pushes her to explain more about what makes her think that, the reader is now forced to deepen her thinking and understanding of the text. Therefore, by talking about texts, students not only are enjoying the chance to talk and build relationships with peers, they also are working on constructing the text in meaningful ways. In addition,

Figure 9-1.

as students grow more proficient in talking about their thinking, I hope their thinking itself gets deeper and more coherent.

Talking about books not only gives the readers a nudge into deepening and clarifying their thinking about the text, but it also gives me insights into the ways they construct meaning from the texts. The talk allows me to coach and confer into their meaning-making in genuine ways. Coaching into readers' natural talk offers me this authentic experience and motivates readers to want to learn how to talk about books with their friends in more sophisticated ways.

WHY CONFER DURING TALK TIME

- It offers more opportunities to confer with readers throughout the week.
- I can assess comprehension and reading skills during conversations.
- I can support multiple readers at one time.

Researching Partnerships and Book Clubs

Just like during one-on-one conferring, I usually begin my research by observing the readers at work. I stand back so I can see what the readers are doing naturally. During this time I also reread my conferring records. I might ask myself:

- "Are the students using the strategies I taught them during our previous conferences or minilessons?"
- "What behaviors and strategies are they using?"
- "What are these readers still struggling with?"

While looking for answers to my questions, I jot down in my conferring records what I am noticing.

During this research phase I have many choices to make, but one of the most important decisions is whether I am going to focus on reading skills and strategies, conversational skills and strategies, or both at once. To help make this decision, I pay attention to both the reading skills and the conversational skills that I see them using while I research. For example, if I want to research how two students are navigating longer texts now that they have transitioned into chapter books, I observe and listen to their talk about their books while thinking about how they are making sense of the characters over time and how they are connecting the plot in one chapter to the next. I still ask myself the same questions—"What new strategies are they using and what are they struggling with?"—but I focus on their reading strategies. In addition, I can observe and notice how the listener is positioning himself, if he responds to the speaker's ideas or simply moves to his own agenda, or how well prepared the readers are for their talk. I ask myself the same assessment questions, but they focus on conversational strategies. In many cases I begin my research by noticing both the reading and conversational skills students are using and decide from the observations what I want to focus on.

Recently, I approached a pair of second-grade students talking about their series books. Each reader held a *Cam Jansen* book in his hands, and Tommy was explaining his prediction about how the crime was going to be solved. He explained his reasoning and said, "So that is what I think is going to happen." His partner Susan smiled and said, "I agree." The conversation came to a halt and the two just sat staring at each other. As they were talking, I asked myself, "What reading skills and what conversational skills do I see that they are using, and what skills do I need to teach them?" Specifically, "Are they forming their own ideas and sharing them? Are they able to add on to each other's ideas? Are they making connections to other books in this series?" While I did notice Tommy was able to form an idea (a prediction) and explain it to his partner, I really didn't see much evidence of Susan adding on to the idea or of either reader making connections to the other *Cam Jansen* books they had just finished reading. I decided to compliment how Tommy shared his prediction and to teach them how to make connections to other books in a series. I made this decision because I almost always make reading skills the priority when both reading and conversational skills could be taught.

Questions I Might Consider as I Research Partnerships and Book Clubs	
Researching Reading Skills	**Researching Conversational Skills**
■ Are readers making connections between this text and other texts? Between this text and themselves?	■ Are readers asking each other to clarify their ideas?
■ Are readers simply summarizing the text or forming an idea?	■ Are readers asking each other to provide examples and evidence?
■ What are students doing once they have formed an idea? Providing evidence? Looking for alternative explanations?	■ When readers are reading the same book or a book about the same character, are they adding on to each other's ideas?
■ How are students dealing with parts of the text that do not align with their ideas?	■ Are readers able to discuss conflicting ideas with respect?
■ Are students focusing solely on characters or are they using other story elements?	■ Are readers using their notes to prepare for the conversation?

Deciding What to Teach

After researching the partnership or club, I make a decision about which skill to teach. Usually I find readers are struggling with more than one skill, so I choose one skill that I believe is within the readers' grasp. If they are approximating a skill and need a nudge, I choose to support that skill. If readers feel stuck and need a new way to talk or think about books, I choose a new skill to teach and offer a strategy for being able to do this skill.

Once I have chosen a skill to teach, I have to think of a strategy I can teach for how to do that skill. While many of my decisions will be based on the whole-class study or reading level of the group, these decisions also can be made based on what I observe during the conversation. The table that follows is one I developed to help make decisions about what skills and strategies I can teach the readers about their talk.

When Readers Are Struggling With These Conversational Skills . . .	I Can Teach Them to . . .
Sticking to one idea	▪ Restate the first idea and then either ask a question, add an example, or ask for more evidence before moving to the next idea. ▪ Ask if anyone has anything else to say about the idea before moving on. ▪ Make a list of all the ideas they want to discuss and then talk about one at a time.
Having a conversation that's worth having	Before having the conversation ask themselves if it is really worth having: ▪ Is it important in the larger context of the book? ▪ Does it force them to synthesize or put together what they have read so far? ▪ Will it lead to a deeper interpretation or idea? ▪ Will it cause them to rethink an idea?
Advancing an idea	▪ Read for evidence that supports or contradicts the idea. ▪ Take notes with a focus on just that idea, jotting down all the parts that add to the idea.
Providing evidence for ideas	▪ Find the part of the book that makes them think that. Use Post-its to keep track of the parts.
Being able to listen	▪ Wait for the speaker to finish, then add on. ▪ Jot a note to themselves about their idea while the speaker finishes so they won't forget it.

Teaching Methods for Conference During Talk Time

After observing partners or clubs from afar, I move closer so I really can hear and take note of what the readers are saying. I do not position myself as another member of the group right away. Instead I stand behind the group or partners and observe silently. I must decide at this point whether the group needs me to stop the conversation and do some explicit teaching or whether they just need a nudge to get back on track or lift the level of the conversation.

Once I have done some research, I decide which method I will use to teach in the conference. I usually rely on one of three methods: ghost partner (a form of coaching), demonstration, or proficient partner (Calkins 2001). My decision about which method to choose depends on a number of factors, such as what strategy I want to teach, how much support I think the readers need, and the dynamics of the group.

Ghost-Partner Teaching

Ghost partnering is when I am not physically a part of the group and, therefore, I do not speak to the whole group myself. I coined the term *ghost partner,* which is described in *The Art of Teaching Reading* as "whispering in" (Calkins 2001), because I want to be as invisible as possible while I coach the group. I support the group members by whispering prompts into their ears and allowing them to continue ownership over the conversation. This allows readers to learn the conversational language and have a successful conversation. When I become the ghost partner, I am supporting both the listener by giving him language to use for how to talk to the speaker and the speaker by giving him the language for how to communicate an idea to the group.

One September morning I listened to Karen retell her book to her partner, Simone. Karen explained, "In this book the author is describing all the stuff that happened to this girl and the girl kept getting into trouble and then she got mad and finally she became good." I saw Simone struggling to follow Karen's vague retelling. Simone responded by using a conversational prompt and said, "I don't really get what your book was about. Can you say it a different way?" There was a long pause and Karen kept looking at her book and flipping through the pages.

I wanted to help Karen by telling her that in a conversation a speaker sometimes starts by retelling what happened in the beginning of the book, then the middle, and then the end. But this was a minilesson I recently had taught to the whole class. Instead of reteaching the minilesson to her, I simply whispered the conversational prompt into her ear:"In the beginning of this book. . . ." Karen repeated the prompt and continued by retelling the beginning events. When she got stuck again, I whispered to her, "In the middle of this book. . . ." Again, Karen was able to tell the middle events and, by the time she finished, she was able to say for herself, "And at the end of the book. . . ." By being a ghost partner for Karen, I enabled her to use some conversational language while maintaining ownership of the successful conversation with her partner.

In a fourth-grade classroom where I was working with a group of teachers on conferring, I noticed a partnership that was reading their ideas from their Post-it notes to each other without stopping to talk about them. I decided that I wanted to help them focus on one idea before moving to the next idea, but I needed to choose how I wanted to teach this. I began by listening to them read off the Post-its to each other and took note of the questions that came to my mind as a listener. When Pablo said, "I think that the boy is scared and kind of angry," I was thinking in my head, "What makes you think that?" Instead of jumping in and becoming the third member of their partnership, I whispered into his partner Thelma's ear, "Ask him: 'What makes you think that?'" Thelma repeated the question to Pablo, who was jolted out of his notes-reading and forced to deepen his thinking for his partner.

The teaching decision that I made was to concentrate on the conversational skill of focusing on one idea before moving to the next. The skill of supporting an idea with evidence from the text also was reinforced through the talk. I decided to support their conversation by being a ghost partner and allowing the readers to continue the conversation with minimal interruptions.

By deciding to serve as a ghost partner, I can help students maintain ownership of the conversation while still supporting them to continue to improve their conversational language and strategies. When choosing to use a ghost-partner method, I consider a few things about the readers in the partnership, such as whether the readers are attempting to use reading and conversational strategies with limited success and whether they have the foundations of a basic conversation. I look to see if the conversation lacks a focused idea and whether partners are pushing each other for deeper thinking. I choose to be a ghost partner who supports either the speaker or listener with conversational language and behaviors to help readers deepen their thinking about their books.

Sample Prompt Menu for Supporting Reading Skills Through Conversation

When Readers Need Help With ...	I Can Prompt Them to Say ...
Envisioning	"I am picturing . . ."
Clarifying	"I don't understand. What is a . . . ?"
	"What does that mean?"
Retelling	"My book was about . . . "
	"In the beginning . . . , then in the middle . . . , and at the end . . ."
Inferring	"This is making me think . . ."
	"I think the character is doing that because . . ."
Predicting	"So far I know . . . and that makes me think . . . will happen next."

Demonstration Teaching

While I try to start with the least amount of interruption in my conferences, which often is achieved through prompting students in a ghost-partner role, there are times when students need me to stop the conversation and do some explicit teaching. I usually make the decision to stop a conversation if the readers are not talking, not responding to each other at all, not pushing each other to deepen their thinking, or not prepared to have the conversation. Basically, I make the decision to stop a conversation when I think whispering prompts will not be supportive enough to help the readers. I notice whether the readers actually are talking or simply are staring at their books or each other. I notice whether the readers get quiet when I approach them or drastically change their behaviors, and I notice whether the readers look comfortable with each other. Finally, I notice whether the readers are prepared for the conversation with parts, ideas, or thoughts to discuss.

If students are struggling with the behaviors and strategies listed above, then I generally choose to do some explicit teaching and not use the ghost-partner method. I choose explicit teaching through demonstration when readers are struggling with the most basic and fundamental aspects of having a conversation, such as coming prepared to talk, sitting with eye contact and facing one another, being able to start the conversation, or having the confidence to talk in front of others.

Once I decide to teach explicitly through demonstration, I stop the conversation and ask for the readers' attention. Just as I do in my one-on-one conferences, I give the readers an explicit compliment either about their conversational skills, their conversational behaviors, or their reading skills.

Compliment Menu for Conversational Skills and Behaviors	
Possible Skills to Compliment Focused on Conversational Behaviors	**Possible Skills to Compliment Focused on Conversational Skills**
Facing each other and making eye contact	Responding to what the speaker just said
Taking turns to speak	Asking clarifying questions
Coming to the conversation prepared to talk	Supporting an idea
Speaking in quiet voices that do not disrupt others	Offering advice to the speaker, such as rereading a section
Having all of their materials ready to talk	Offering an alternative idea

Once I give the compliment, I move to stating the teaching point. I make sure to address both partners in my teaching, but I may choose to demonstrate by acting as a partner myself and using one of the other readers as my demonstration partner.

One afternoon I approached Andy and Tyrell during partner talk time and noticed that while Andy had a few Post-its in his book and was prepared for the conversation, Tyrell had nothing prepared and, therefore, was not able to participate easily in the conversation. I listened as Andy said to Tyrell, "What are you thinking about Cam right now?" Tyrell flipped through the pages of the first two chapters and said, "He is trying to figure out who stole the baseball." Andy responded by saying, "I know that. You told me that yesterday. What are you *thinking* about Cam so far?" "Well . . . ," Tyrell sputtered as he flipped back through the pages again. At this point I needed to intervene. I did enough research to decide this was a nice opportunity to show the two readers why it is so important to prepare for a conversation and demonstrate a way to prepare.

"Can I stop you for a few minutes?" I said to the two boys. They nodded and put their books down. Andy looked a little relieved. "First, I want to compliment you. When I came over and watched you talking, I noticed that you were sticking to one reader's idea before moving to another. I saw that you were talking about Cam in Tyrell's book and, even though it was kind of a struggle, you didn't give up and jump to Andy's ideas. Readers know that when they talk about books, they should stick to one idea before moving to anther. Good work! Keep doing that whenever you talk about your books." The two boys smiled and sat up a little taller.

After giving the compliment I moved to stating the problem and teaching point. "I noticed that you were kind of getting stuck in your conversation. Andy, you were asking Tyrell questions about Cam, and he kept flipping through the pages and didn't really tell you anything new." Andy and Tyrell nodded. "I want to teach you how important it is to come to your conversations prepared to talk, and that one way to prepare is to take a few notes at the parts of your book that get you thinking about your character. Then you can use those notes to jog your memory and get you started when you talk." I took out the class read-aloud we were in the middle of reading, *Nate the Great* by Marjorie Shermat, and turned back to the last chapter we had read. "I would like you two to watch me as I read a little and then stop and ask myself, 'What am I thinking about Nate right now?' Then I will jot a few words about my thinking on a Post-it note and stick it right next to the part that gave me the idea." I proceeded to read, think aloud, and take a few notes.

When I finished, I restated the teaching point and explained to them why being prepared with notes is so important. "So, whenever you are reading and your character does something or says something that gives you an idea, you can jot a few notes on a Post-it and bring those notes to your conversations. Your conversation will go much better by having those notes to talk off of. And what you talk about might even give you a new idea to take notes about during the next part of your reading."

Then I set them up to get started on this skill. "I would like you to take out your books and reread the last page or two. Push yourself to get an idea and then write it on this Post-it note." I placed a Post-it on each of their books and observed as Andy quickly jotted a note on his page. "Great, Andy! Keep going while Tyrell prepares to talk." I looked at Tyrell, who said, "Right here, Cam is noticing a clue. I am going to jot a note about that." "Great, Tyrell!" I said. The two boys then agreed to stop and read some more and take some notes before having their next conversation. I reminded them to hold each other accountable to come prepared to talk and that if one or both of them were not prepared, they shouldn't have the conversation.

In this conference I identified a problem that arose during the partners' talk and used that as a springboard for my teaching. I decided to stop and do some demonstrating because Tyrell was not prepared for the talk and, therefore, the discussion could not continue. I also noticed a pattern in Tyrell and Andy's conversations during the last conferences with them. I noticed their writing about reading was very scarce. I decided that simply telling them to take notes would not have been supportive enough for them. The teaching part of the conference followed an architecture similar to that of a one-on-one demonstration, yet I was able to ask the two of them to hold each other accountable for what I taught them.

Proficient-Partner Teaching

Sometimes I observe a conversation and notice that readers are going through the motions of having a conversation, but they are not pushing themselves or their partners to deepen their thinking. Oftentimes before readers really have internalized the conversational strategies, they spend so much time thinking about what to say and how to participate that they do not really focus on what is most important: deepening and growing their ideas. In this case I may decide to become another member of their group to push the conversation in a more productive direction. To do so, I simply sit down in the group and participate in the conversation by asking questions, offering insights, and adding on to other ideas. I do not stop the conversation; I just step into it. This is a little more supportive than the ghost partnership because I actually am helping to lead the conversation. The conversation and thinking take a different turn thanks to my presence as the proficient partner because I am guiding the content and showing the students new strategies. At the end of the conversation, I tend to stop and explicitly state for the group what I just did and suggest that they try to do it from now on.

Other times I notice a conversation is really strong and the readers are using all the strategies they have been taught. I may choose to become a proficient partner in order to push them to continue deepening their work or to join in on the great conversation.

One January afternoon, I observed a third-grade classroom of students who were just learning to work in book clubs. This was the club's second book in the *Junie B. Jones* series by Barbara Park, but the conversation was still on the surface level. After listening to the club stay for a few minutes on the idea that Junie is silly, I decided to become a proficient partner because the conversation was not really going anywhere. Lacey stated, "She is also silly in the part when she really believes that there is a monster under her bed." "Yeah," Riccardo agreed. I sat down and offered another idea. "While I agree that Junie is silly, I also think she can be really smart. Sometimes she is silly and sometimes she is smart. She is both. What do you think about that?" I saw a few heads nodding and then Lacey said, "I agree that she can be smart." "Like when in the other book she . . . , " Ashley interrupted to add. They talked about this idea for a while and then I spoke up again. "I also think Junie can be naughty. Like when she didn't listen to her grandma and made a mess with the cereal." The other members of the club laughed and added other examples of when she was naughty.

As the conversation came to an end, I stopped the group and summarized what I was doing. "So, readers, whenever we seemed stuck on one idea about Junie I redirected us by offering another idea about her. I did this because, just like real people, characters are not just one way. We can and should discuss more than one idea about a character. Do you think that you all can do this from now on? You can redirect the conversation to another idea about the character when you notice you are getting stuck." They nodded and I stepped back as they continued to talk.

I've learned from Lucy Calkins that when I'm being a proficient partner, I can give extra support to readers who need it or push readers who are already proficient to deepen their strategies. In this proficient-partner conference, I participated in the conversation by authentically modeling how the conversation could go. I tried to deepen their talk and their thinking by pushing them to leave an idea after they started repeating the same things over and over again. I also offered them a new strategy, which was to notice that characters are not just one way and that we can discuss more than one idea about a character in a book. After doing this as a part of the club, I summarized the strategies for the group so that they could continue the work independently.

Deciding Which Method to Use

While there is no wrong decision about which conferring teaching method to choose, some methods set up readers to work independently more than others. I recommend using the least amount of support—for example, whispering into readers' ears in a ghost-partner method—first. If readers still need more support, stop them and demonstrate the strategy. If you recognize that you are spending a lot of time acting as the proficient partner in conversations, try to use demonstration or become a ghost partner, thus offering students less support to push for independence. Knowing the dynamics of the partnerships and clubs well helps me ultimately make my decision.

Methods of Teaching	Characteristics
Ghost partner	■ The teacher does not become an overt part of the conversation. ■ The teacher coaches the readers by whispering prompts into their ears as the talk continues. ■ Students maintain ownership of all the talk in the group.
Demonstration	■ The teacher stops the group, names the strategy she is teaching, and demonstrates the strategy. ■ The teacher gets the readers to try the strategy quickly. ■ The teacher names the strategy and asks readers to keep using it independently.
Proficient partner	■ The teacher becomes a member of the conversational group. ■ The teacher models the strategies she wants the group to use. ■ The teacher names the strategies she modeled and asks readers to keep using them.

Balancing Individual and Talk Conferences

After much daily practice, I typically have anywhere from three to five one-on-one conferences and three to five conferences during talk time in an hour-long reading workshop. The trick is to balance the time and focus of my conferences so that readers are benefiting from both individual conferences that are specifically geared to their unique needs and frequent talk-time conferences that support their reading, talking, and thinking. The key to my success is keeping clear records that document my teaching methods, content, and structures. Using partner talk and club time to confer with readers about their thinking and talking helps me meet with readers more frequently and gives me a more holistic picture of what students think about as they read and talk about books.

Classroom Applications

- Choose a partnership and study it for a few days. Take notes and transcribe what the students say and do when they talk. Then bring these notes to a grade-level meeting and discuss what you could compliment and teach the partnership.
- Step back and observe a partnership and try becoming the ghost partner. Don't become a third partner, but instead whisper the prompts you want to say to one of the readers. Let the partners try out your suggestions for themselves.
- Practice your demonstration teaching with a partnership or club. Remember the structure is the same as an individual-demonstration conference.
- Participate in a conversation by becoming a proficient partner. Model conversational or reading strategies for students. Remember to name the strategy at the end of the conference so students can replicate it when you are gone.
- Videotape a strong partner conversation or book club and watch it with colleagues. Think about what strengths the group has in terms of both conversational skills and reading skills. Then create a strategy overview based on what you saw so you can teach others to do the same things.

Planning for What to Teach and How to Teach It

10

"Before beginning a Hunt, it is wise to ask someone what you are looking for before you begin looking for it."

— WINNIE THE POOH, A. A. MILNE

In my first yoga class, I watched as my instructor made his forearms into a triangle on the ground, put his head in between them, and went upside down into a headstand. He then crossed his feet over the tops of his thighs and bent them forward so that his knees touched his elbows. I stood staring and thought, "That's magic. The human body is not meant to contort itself in such a way. There is no way I will ever be able to do that." Over the past ten years that I've been practicing yoga, I have learned that a lot of the poses that at first seemed magical (including the "inverted bound lotus headstand" described earlier) are, in fact, not magic. Granted, I still can't do that one but I have learned that most poses were within my reach once I knew what poses to practice and how to practice them.

Reading conferring is a lot like yoga. Those who are excellent at it seem to be performing magic. I remember watching Lucy Calkins, Carl Anderson, and Amanda Hartman model conferences in my classroom. I watched them in awe the way I watched my yoga instructors and thought, "Wow! How did Lucy know the exact right thing to teach Luis? How did Carl have that book at his fingertips that was perfect for that example? Amanda's demonstration was so perfect, it looks almost like it's been rehearsed."

What I now know is that, as with yoga, what seemed like magic actually wasn't. Lucy knew what to teach Luis because she knows so much about what good reading looks like that she can be on the lookout for when students exhibit or contradict those behaviors. Carl was able to have ready a perfect text to use in a conference because he has a few texts that he knows very well that he uses again and again in conferences. And Amanda had no trouble doing an excellent demonstration because she draws from what she knows about good teaching. In other words, all of these teachers had planned or prepared, to some extent, before sitting down next to my students.

Although conferring seems spontaneous, or conversation-like, I need to be prepared—and the way to prepare is not unlike how I prepared in yoga to do the inverted bound lotus headstand. Just as my teacher broke down inverted bound lotus headstand into its component parts (learning how to build upper-body strength for the headstand, developing flexibility in my hips for the lotus position, understanding how to practice with patience and proper breathing), conferring can be broken down into its component parts. In other words, it's important I know *what* to teach in a conference and *how* to teach it. This means knowing how to come up with a bank of teaching points, but also having conferences for individuals thought out ahead of time.

Conferring is not magic; it's within reach of everyone.

Develop a Repertoire of What to Teach in a Conference

To achieve my goal of learning the inverted bound lotus headstand, I knew there were certain poses that I needed to practice. I needed to be able to do a headstand well. I needed to be able to do bound lotus while sitting on the ground. I needed to know *what* to practice.

Likewise in conferring, I need to know *what* to teach. I need to have a repertoire of possible strategies that I'm able to access at a moment's notice. I also need to be skilled at assessing wisely to match those strategies to different readers.

Mining Your Own Reading of a Genre for What to Teach

When I read a lot, in many genres, and am able to reflect on myself as a reader, it helps me to become a better reading workshop teacher. When I am able to read the beginning of a short story, for example, and spy on myself as I read, I can come up with a menu of strategies that can be applied to my conferences with students. What I teach students to do in a reading workshop is really just a broken-down, clearly articulated version of strategies that I, as a proficient reader, naturally integrate into all of my reading.

Try it. As you read this passage from the short story "The Gift of the Magi," by O. Henry, notice what helps you to comprehend the text. What do you do when your comprehension starts to break down? Do you find yourself having ideas about the characters? How did you arrive at those ideas? As you read, line by line, try to mark up the text to show your thinking.

Excerpt from "The Gift of the Magi"

by O. Henry

One dollar and eighty-seven cents. That was all. And sixty cents of it was in pennies. Pennies saved one and two at a time by bulldozing the grocer and the vegetable man and the butcher until one's cheeks burned with the silent imputation of parsimony that such close dealing implied. Three times Della counted it. One dollar and eighty-seven cents. And the next day would be Christmas.

There was clearly nothing to do but flop down on the shabby little couch and howl. So Della did it. Which instigates the moral reflection that life is made up of sobs, sniffles, and smiles, with sniffles predominating.

While the mistress of the home is gradually subsiding from the first stage to the second, take a look at the home. A furnished flat at $8 per week. It did not exactly beggar description, but it certainly had that word on the lookout for the mendicancy squad. In the vestibule below was a letter-box into which no letter would go, and an electric button from which no mortal finger could coax a ring. Also appertaining thereunto was a card bearing the name "Mr. James Dillingham Young."

As a proficient reader, you might have begun by imagining the scene and its characters from the very first paragraph. You perhaps developed images in your mind of Della—at the grocer, the vegetable stand, and the butcher, with coins in her hand, and at home, plopped down on the couch with tears starting to roll down her cheeks. You no doubt started to see the environment in which Della was sitting, and you probably started to make judgments about her as a character. Maybe you asked yourself questions like, "I wonder why she has found herself in such a shabby apartment, with so little money, grasping onto just pennies?" Perhaps you thought a bit about her as a character, beginning to wonder why she had such a negative outlook on life—"with sniffles predominating"—and what kind of a person she was to be so worried about saving up enough money for Christmas. Perhaps you got to the word *mendicancy* and reread the sentence, trying to figure out what it meant.

You probably realized that you integrated several skills into your reading of just a few paragraphs. You envisioned (made mental pictures of the people and the setting), you predicted (asked yourself questions and wondered what would come next), you inferred (when you came up with ideas about the character), and you used a fix-up strategy (when you realized you didn't know the meaning of a word). Good readers utilize all of these skills and more as they read, and, in a reading workshop, it is up to us to make this all visible to the student, one strategy at a time.

Figure 10-1 shows my version of this text, marked up to show my thinking as I read.

When trying to figure out *what* to teach in a reading conference, it is often helpful for me to be able to notice what it is that *I* do in order to comprehend the text. The more practiced I become at being aware of myself as a reader, the more skills and strategies I have available to use during conferences to help my students become better readers.

Steps to Mining Your Own Reading for What to Teach

■ Choose an adult-level text of the genre you want your students to read.
■ Read and mark up the text profusely with your thoughts and reading behaviors.
■ Go back and analyze your thoughts in light of the reading skills.
■ Assign a strategy to each idea you had by asking yourself, "How did I get that idea?"
■ Use what you've learned about your own reading as strategies to teach your students.

Excerpt from *Gift Of The Magi*

by O. Henry

One dollar and eighty-seven cents. That was all. And sixty cents

→ what does she do for a living?

of it was in pennies. Pennies saved one and two at a time by

bulldozing the grocer and the vegetable man and the butcher until

who?

one's cheeks burned with the silent imputation of parsimony that such — ?

close dealing implied. Three times Della counted it. One dollar and

eighty-seven cents. And the next day would be Christmas.

I can understand how she must feel — disappointed, nervous, embarrassed

There was clearly nothing to do but flop down on the shabby little

I can picture and hear this

couch and howl. So Della did it. Which instigates the moral

reflection that life is made up of sobs, sniffles, and smiles, with

sniffles predominating. Is this the author's viewpoint of life, really? How depressing.

While the mistress of the home is gradually subsiding from the first

→ now I'm thinking this was a long time ago, and maybe in England?

stage to the second, take a look at the home. A furnished flat at $8

per week. It did not exactly beggar description, but it certainly — ?

had that word on the lookout for the mendicancy squad. In the

re-read here — got lost.

vestibule below was a letter-box into which no letter would go, and

an electric button from which no mortal finger could coax a ring.

Also appertaining thereunto was a card bearing the name "Mr. James

what relation is this man to her? Father? Husband? Roommate?

Dillingham Young."

Figure 10-1. A marked-up copy showing my thinking as I read.

Studying Text Levels for What to Teach

In Chapter 7, I wrote about creating conferring menus based on text-level difficulties to help with researching and teaching in a reading conference. This section offers more detailed help in how to do that.

When I sit down next to a student in a reading conference, I research to learn what the student is doing that day and how the student is using strategies that have been learned in past conferences and minilessons. But what I also do is take a look at the student's book. I research the book. I attempt to notice what the text difficulties might be, and use what I notice to ask purposeful questions to find out how the student is handling those difficulties.

While researching the book, I look for text difficulties and qualities of the text that appear in many books. I might have questions in my mind, such as:

- What do I notice about the density of text on the page?
- What do I notice about the way(s) in which the pictures do or do not support comprehension?
- What do I notice about the complexity of vocabulary on the page?
- What do I notice about sentence length and sentence structure?
- What do I notice about the way that the text is written that might affect fluency or intonation?

I use my answers to these questions to define the characteristics of books at this level. For example, let's say that I want to study Irene Fountas and Gay Su Pinnell's level K. Some examples of texts at this level include *Nate the Great,* by Marjorie Weinman Sharmat; *Meet M&M,* by Pat Ross; and *The Smallest Cow in the World,* by Katherine Paterson. From studying a few books at this level, I can generalize that texts of this level tend to have the following characteristics:

- Frequent use of dialogue that helps to move the plot along
- Extended descriptions
- Episodic chapters, with each chapter contributing to the understanding of the entire book
- Limited picture support—pictures often appear on different pages than the corresponding text or may even tell a different story than the text
- Challenging and unusual vocabulary

The next step in planning my teaching points is taking each of these characteristics and naming skills a reader would need to use to handle that characteristic or difficulty. In order to comprehend in parts where the dialogue is dense, for example, a reader at this level would have to be able to *envision* the scene to keep track of the dialogue. In addition, frequent stretches of dialogue require that the reader is able to *read with expression,* taking into account the personalities of the different characters.

The last step is to preplan strategies that I might teach. Whenever I plan strategies, I like to have a collection because I know a strategy that works for one reader might not work for another, and because sometimes there are strategies that help a reader to work more deeply at one skill. To plan out strategies, I often look back at the part of the text that demands the skill and ask myself, "Well, how would *I* do it?" Then I state my skill with the word *by* and then a step-by-step procedure of a way to do it. For example, if I want to envision the scene, I might go back to a place with a long stretch of dialogue and ask, "How would *I* do it?" I could come up with a few possibilities. I envision the scene *by* picturing the two people who are having the conversation and looking back and forth between them in my mind. I also envision the scene *by* using what I know about the characters to be able to determine who says what. I also envision the scene *by* having different voices for each of the characters in my head, and hearing the different voices as I read.

STEPS TO STUDYING TEXT LEVELS FOR WHAT TO TEACH

- Look at a text, asking yourself questions about what might pose difficulties to a reader. Write down what you notice.
- Look at the list of text difficulties and determine what reading skill would help the reader to handle each difficulty.
- Come up with a list of strategies to go with each skill. Do this by rereading the part of the text and asking yourself, "How would *I* do it?"
- State your teaching points as the skill + the word *by* + the strategy for doing it.

Researching with Knowledge of Text Levels in Mind

Knowing the characteristics of the text helps me to quickly scan the page the student is reading to ascertain whether he is able to handle the difficulty.

When I research with knowledge of text difficulties, I let the research of the text inform my research of the *student*. Because of what I notice about the text, I might ask the reader research questions such as:

- "What's been happening in this part of the book [when there is a large section of dialogue]?"
- "What picture are you getting in your mind as you read this [descriptive] paragraph?"
- "How do all of the chapters that you've read so far fit together?"
- "How are you using the pictures to help you with your understanding of what you've read?"
- "Can you point to a word that was new for you and tell me how you figured out what that word means?"

In many cases, I will find that one of these text characteristics has posed a certain challenge for the reader, and I then am able to determine a conference teaching point based on that assessment.

I often find it helpful to have a one-page menu of everything I've planned. Usually this menu has a list of characteristics of a leveled text, questions to ask to assess the student's understanding of that level, and possible teaching points that would stem from the assessment, like the one in Chapter 7. (For more information on text characteristics by level, see books by Fountas and Pinnell [1999; 2001; 2005]).

Studying Past Conference Notes for What to Teach

Jayna is a fourth grader who devours books. She's the kind of student who fills her book baggie each week with an ambitious amount of reading, and then zooms through the books all week. As I sat down next to her on one Monday morning, I asked her to tell me a little bit about the books she'd chosen for her reading that week.

"Well, I love this series. The *Junie B. Jones* books are my favorites, so I thought that this week I'd read a lot of them. And then I thought I'd also try one of these *Riverside Kids* books by Joanna Hurwitz because Isabelle told me about them, and she said she thought I'd like the main character, so that's why I picked it."

I quickly glanced over my conference notes with Jayna for the past few weeks. I had written "seems to be reading a lot. Not sure if she's stopping enough to make connections to the text," "strong at literal comprehension," "strong retelling," and "needs to do more inferring about characters." I knew what I could teach.

"Jayna, it's so smart of you to have chosen so many books in the same series. Readers do this all the time. They get to know an author or a series really well and then read a bunch of books by that same author all in a row. You know what? One of the things that's so great about reading in a series is that you get to know the main characters really, really well. Those same main characters show up in all the books, so today I'm going to teach you how you can start to get to know your characters even better by paying attention to character relationships in this book, this book, and this book."

As I confer with students day after day, my understanding of each student as an individual reader takes shape. Every conference is an opportunity to assess my students and to sharpen the image that I have about who they are as readers, and what reading skills and strategies they are using that help them to comprehend and think deeply about texts. I use these assessments to develop individualized plans for students, and these individualized plans will help their conferring become more effortless. I will consider what reading skills I hope my students will be able to master by the end of the month and the end of the school year.

My planning and preparation is not only from general goals I have based on the whole-class study or level; my planning is, to a large extent, specific to the reader with whom I'm working. I think about developing individualized goals.

Let's take, for example, the notes from a series of two conferences with Ramon. Notes from conferences with Ramon on October 10 and October 15 are shown in Figure 10-2. When developing instructional goals for Ramon, I could look across my notes to help me see patterns in what I'd noticed and what I was thinking. I decided that retelling was going to continue to be a goal for my work with him because he didn't demonstrate competency during the October 10 conference, and he needed coaching during the October 15 conference. I also liked that he

Ramon

Compliments I could give the reader	What I could teach the reader
10/10 · uses strategies taught in minilessons ⓒ · uses character action to get an idea about the character · summarizes · provides text evidence · predicts based on knowledge of series	· understanding purpose behind strategies · naming his work as a reader · elaborating on an idea · retelling in sequence ⓣ · getting an idea based on character dialogue
10/15 · continued work of last conference · able to have ideas about characters ⓒ · supports ideas w/ text evidence · sticks to one main character	ⓣ · building a theory about a character by looking across post-its. · needed coaching to retell — tends to summarize

Figure 10-2. Conferring notes from two conferences with the same reader.

demonstrated some inferring by getting ideas about his characters, but I was going to continue to push him to think a little more deeply about his characters, and, in time, apply what he did with one character to multiple characters in his book. I also noticed that Ramon was reading within a series and he started making some connections between books, so now I encouraged him to do more of this kind of work. All of this work helped him think about his books when he was reading independently, and it also helped him when he was working with his partner. I payed close attention to how he talked about his book—both the ideas and the retelling—when he met with his reading partner.

It is important to note that the goal for Ramon has certain qualities to it. These qualities of a good plan based on assessment come from the TCRWP's and Carl Anderson's (2005) work on assessing writers.

First, the goals that I set for Ramon are within his reach. They are goals that a student can perform under minimal adult guidance or with peer collaboration. While it is tempting to have in mind where a student *should* be at a certain grade level and to push that student to hold texts that are too hard and to master skills that are too advanced, teaching students strategies they can do now with slight teacher assistance will be strategies that students soon will be able to do independently. Independence is a constant goal of every workshop teacher. Because Ramon has shown me some evidence that he is able to get ideas about his character, it is a realistic goal for him.

My goals for Ramon are not all over the board. While I do want him to seamlessly integrate all of the skills that I know a reader should be able to do, my individual plan for him is one that tackles a few at a time. It makes more sense to the learner to focus on a few goals over a period of time. He will practice these skills in a variety of contexts until he is able to do them independently and automatically.

The goals I have for him also are influenced both by the current whole-class study, by his reading level, and by what I have noticed about him as a reader. Using multiple sources of information is essential.

Analyzing Running Records for What to Teach

In Chapter 4, I wrote about using running records as a means to match students to just-right books. These documents have a lot of information about the cueing systems that readers use when they encounter difficulty, as well as information about fluency and comprehension. Running records offer so much information about what readers might need next.

Keep in mind that the running records need to have some miscues on them in order to do the following analyses.

Running-Record Miscue Analysis

After completing a running record, I look back at it to analyze what the student does when she encounters difficulty. Running-record analysis is very involved and complex, and what follows should be seen as an introduction to the topic. For more information, I recommend reading Marie Clay's book on running records (2001).

Analysis of running records requires that a teacher make her best inference into what cueing system the reader is probably using. Cueing systems can be seen as strategies students use when figuring out new words. First, it's important to know the three cueing systems that all readers use: meaning (or semantic), syntactic (or sentence structure), and visual (graphophonic). Proficient readers use a combination of these cueing systems in unison as they encounter new words. As proficient readers read, their knowledge of what makes sense, what sounds right, and what looks right all helps them to read the text. When students who are learning to read encounter a new text, they will often encounter difficulty. When I analyze miscues, I am looking to see what the reader *did* use when he encountered difficulty.

When students use the *meaning* (M) cueing system, the word that they read in error means the same thing as the word in the text or matches the picture on the page. If students are using *syntax* (S) to figure out a new word, then their error is the same part of speech as the word in the text (noun for noun, verb for verb, and so forth). When students use *visual* (V), they are relying on the appearance of the letters in the word. Students will often look first at the initial letter or cluster of letters, next at the ending of the word, and finally at the middle of the word.

For example, if a student is reading a sentence that reads, "Her mother asked her to go to the store to get some milk," and the reader says "mom" instead of "mother," I can infer that the reader might have used all three cueing systems. How? First, I ask myself, "Does the word make sense?" Here, I am checking for the first cueing system—meaning, or semantic. Yes, *mom* makes sense in the sentence; it means the same thing as *mother*. Second, I ask, "Does the word sound right?"—that is, is it the same part of speech and syntactically correct? The answer to this question is [...] nouns and sound right as the subject [...] word look right?" The answer to this [...] both have the same first two letters, [...] y looked at the beginning of the word [...] sounded right and made sense in the

[...] student read the word "dad" instead [...] s *dad* make sense? Does *dad* sound [...] instance, the student probably only [...] at is, the word "sounds right" but [...] k the same as *mother*. It could be, [...] ; meaning because it does still make

Handwritten note:

> Meaning, or semantic
> makes sense
> mom – mother
> Sound Right or syntactical
> syntax correct or
> same part of speech
> mom, mother
> Look right
> dad
> only used syntax
> more – only used
> visual

What if the student read the word "more" instead of "mother"? *More* doesn't make sense in the sentence, "Her more asked her to go to the store to get some milk"; it doesn't sound right; but it does look a little like *mother*. In this instance, I would say that the student used the visual, or grapho-phonic, cueing system only.

When analyzing running records, I look for patterns to plan how I will help this student deal with difficulty in her self-chosen books. The important thing to note about this analysis is that it is possible for readers to use one, two, or all three of the cueing systems even when making a single miscue.

After completing an analysis of each miscue and self-correction, I begin to look for patterns and trends. I ask myself:

- What does the student tend to use when encountering a new word?
- When the student self-corrects, what cueing system most likely helped him to self-correct?
- What cueing system(s) is the student not using consistently?

Once I have found the pattern(s), I can use this information to reinforce what the student is using and teach him to use what he is not currently using consistently. I find it helpful to think through each of the three cueing systems and consider different strategies that I could teach the reader to introduce that skill if he isn't using it at all, or to strengthen a skill that he is beginning to use.

For visual, it might mean that I begin with a strategy of "make sure the word looks right *by* making your mouth ready to say the first letter of the word." But it could be that a reader is using the beginning of the word only and making miscues, like "more" instead of "mother" in the example above. In that instance, I might compliment the reader on using the beginning sound of the word, but teach her to "make sure the word looks right *by* looking at the beginning *and* the ending of the word."

Teaching After Miscue Analysis: Strategies and Coaching Prompts

If a Student Is Having Trouble With . . .	Strategies I Could Teach Might Be . . .	Coaching Might Sound Like . . .
Meaning	■ Make sure the word you read makes sense in the sentence by asking yourself, "Does that make sense with what I've read so far?"	■ Does that make sense? ■ Read that again to make sure it makes sense.
Syntax	■ Make sure the word you read sounds right by making sure it is the right part of speech.	■ Does that sound right in the sentence? ■ Does that sound like how it sounds in books?
Visual	■ Make sure the word you read looks right by looking not only at the beginning but also the end of the word.	■ Does that look right? ■ Look all the way through the word to make sure you've said all the sounds.

Running-Record Fluency and Intonation Analysis

In Chapter 4, I wrote about a way to record not only miscues but also fluency and intonation. This information can be used to come up with teaching points for individual students. As when looking at running-record miscues, the first step is to look for some kind of pattern.

When looking at fluency, I often notice if the student tends to pause after a certain number of words, regardless of what the punctuation is telling her to do. I can use this to help me make a decision of what to teach this reader—to help her to sweep her eyes under a few more words than what she is currently doing. For instance, if a reader is reading only one and two words at a time, a good teaching point for a conference would be to help her to sweep her eyes under at least three words at a time.

When looking at intonation, I look again for patterns at the types of punctuation that the student is reading, and the punctuation she is ignoring. In my mind, I look for a few things. First, I want readers to be able to attend to ending punctuation. Second, I want students to be able to phrase their reading as the author intended, which often means paying attention to commas, dashes, semicolons, and colons inside of sentences. Third, I want them to be able to read dialogue with expression.

After looking to see what she is already trying and what my goals are, then I have to decide on the next steps for the reader. I keep in mind that, regardless of what my teaching decision is, I must always teach a strategy for what I want the reader to do. To come up with that strategy, I find it helpful to go to a text that has the same kind of difficulty and read it thinking, "What do *I* do?" For instance, let's say that I have a student who is able to read ending punctuation and phrasing each sentence nicely, paying attention to commas. I might decide to teach her to start reading dialogue in the voice of the character *by* thinking about the way the character is feeling and making her voice sound like that.

Running-Record Comprehension Analysis

At the end of a running record, it is important to ask questions to assess for literal and inferential comprehension. I try to record what the student says on the back of the running record so that I can look at it later for analysis. I look to see the extent to which the reader is able to retell events of the story in sequence, and the extent to which she is able to infer and interpret as she reads. Often, running records are the first piece of data I have about my students' comprehension, so they can be regarded as helpful tools to inform my earliest instruction.

Analyzing Book Logs for What to Teach

In Chapter 3, I talk about the importance of having students keep logs that are a record of what they read, how much time they spend reading, and the number of pages they read in a given amount of minutes. I can analyze these logs to see how long it's taking students to finish books, how much reading they're getting done in school versus at home, the types of books that they like to read, and how long they've been in a particular level. When looking at a log, I might ask the following questions:

- How does the student's reading rate at home vary from his reading rate at school?
- How long is the student reading in school and at home each day?
- How long was this student in one reading level before moving on to the next?
- Does the student tend to read one book at a time, juggle a few books at once, or abandon books before finishing them?
- What genre is the student reading?
- Does the student ever reread?

For example, I recently studied the book logs of students in Amanda Ortiz's third-grade class. One student's log is shown in Figure 10-3.

Khrystyna

17

Reading Levels	Book Title	Date	Reading Location (School or Home)	Start Time	End Time	Page you started on and ended on	How many pages did you read this time?	Teacher/Parent Guardian Comments & Signature
M	Chrysanthemum	9/5/06	School	9:15	9:45	15-32	17	Mrs. Ortiz - Excellent!
L	Don't sit on my lunch!	1-3-07	home	5:47	6:00	24-35	12	
L	Don't sit on my lunch	1-4-07	school	8:45	9:15	33-51	30	
L	Tooth Trouble	1-5-07	home	7:14	7:50	13-90	74	
L	Talent show sleepover books	1-5-07	school	9:15	9:15	1-38	32	
M	Judy Blume	11-5-08	school	2:45	2:45	1-27	12	
M	Judy Blume	1-5-07	home	5:21	5:36	27-39	20	
M	Judy Blume Russ	11-6-07	home	6:00	7:00	33-50	10	
M	Rip-Roaring Russell	1-7-07	home	12:05	12:36	1-23	17	
M	Fish Face	11-8-07	school	8:30	9:15	1-38	18	
M	Fish Face	1-8-07	home	5:00	7:00	38-75	38	

Mrs. Ortiz's Class
3-412
P.S. 63M

Figure 10-3. Khrystyna's book log from one week of reading at home and school.

From studying Khrystyna's log, I see that she reads every night at home for at least a half hour. I notice that on days when she's finishing a book (on January 4 she read for forty-five minutes, and on January 8 for two hours), it's not unusual to see her reading for an hour or two! I have a hunch that she's a reader who, once she gets into a book, will read straight through until it's done. I also can see that her reading rate is inconsistent. On January 6, she reports reading for an hour, but she only read ten pages. But on January 8, she read thirty-eight pages of *Fish Face* at home in the same amount of time. I can also see that she's choosing to read many series books, but doesn't read several books within one series—she jumps from one series to the next. I can see that she is not really someone who rereads because she starts on the next page each time she reads. In addition, she sometimes juggles a few books at once (like when she was reading *Don't Sit on My Lunch* and, after finishing it, restarted reading *Tooth Trouble* from page 13 to the end).

After looking at a student's book logs during a conference or in preparation for a conference, I plan for what to teach based on what I notice. For Khrystyna, I could talk to her about what the conditions are when she's able to read a lot, to see if we can replicate those conditions more often. I could talk to her about her book choice, and perhaps suggest reading several books within a series to help support her moving to a new level. I also would be sure to compliment her on how diligent she is with reading at home and in school every day. To come up with these teaching points, I think about what would help the student to increase volume, stamina, rate, and consistency.

ANALYZING BOOK LOGS FOR WHAT TO TEACH

- Look at a student's book logs for patterns using a set of questions that relate to volume, stamina, rate, and consistency.
- Make a teaching decision based on what would help the reader to improve in any one of these areas.

Planning for How to Teach

In my quest to master the inverted bound lotus headstand, I needed to know more than what poses to practice. Doing these poses improperly would not lead to flexibility, dexterity, and agility; doing them improperly would, most likely, lead to injury. I needed to know *how* to practice the poses. Likewise, in conferring, I need to know *how* to teach. Teaching strategies improperly probably won't injure my students, but I may spend a lot of time without getting my desired results. Knowing how to teach will help my teaching stick, and will help keep my conferences short so that I can see many students within one workshop period.

In this section, I discuss certain ways to prepare how to teach in a conference. I can rely on a predictable structure to help to make my teaching effective and efficient. I can get to know one text exceptionally well by planning how I would use this text in my demonstrations, and be prepared to confer with a "text under the arm" (Anderson 2000). Finally, I can repeat planned demonstrations from minilessons and strategy lessons, and draw from my choices of teaching methods (demonstration, proficient partner, shared reading, coaching) in a conference.

Know the Structure of a Conference

In terms of preparing and planning for conferences, I can work on internalizing a structure. Just as I initially might script out lessons in order to internalize their structure, I also can write out conferences. When I was first learning to confer, I would tape-record my work with students and transcribe my conferences. Then, I'd see if I had all the parts—research, compliment, teach, and link. Often, I'd work with other colleagues in a study group. I might ask myself such questions as:

- Is there any part of the conference that seems to go on too long?
- Is there a good balance of teacher talk and student talk?
- Is the language I used in the demonstration clear?
- Did I coach the student with the leanest prompts possible?
- What indication did the student give me that he was able to try out this strategy independently?

Sometimes, I also write out hypothetical conferences that I might have with students in order to see the structure. The logic behind this is that if I could sit down at a computer and type out a conference, I'd have the benefit of taking my time and thinking about it when I'm not in the heat of the moment. I have found that although at first this feels a bit tedious, it pays off in terms of my ability to confer efficiently as I sit next to a reader.

Reuse Planned Demonstrations from Past Teaching

Many of the demonstrations that we pull into our conferences are demonstrations that we have planned, and done, before. This does not mean that when I do a minilesson on getting an idea about a character based on how he talks to other characters, I should then go out into the classroom and repeat the demonstration six times to individual students. Conferring is my opportunity to individualize and, if I teach the same thing to everyone, there's no individualization. What it does mean is that what I taught on Monday in a minilesson, one-on-one conference, or small-group conference may be an appropriate conference for a student on Wednesday, and that I can reuse my demonstration and demonstration materials to teach an individual student. I often also can reuse think alouds from the planned read-aloud as well, and prepared texts that I know well from shared reading.

I find it wise always to enter conferences thinking about how a student is using not only what I've taught today, not only what I've taught that week, not only what I've taught in that whole class study, but really what I've taught for the entire year so far and what he's demonstrated he can do based on my goals for him. There are times when something that I'm planning to do as a minilesson later that month or that year for the class may be something that is appropriate for one student today.

Sometimes, as I work to internalize the structure and fine-tune my demonstration teaching, I might decide to repeat a conference with the same teaching point several times. This learning time is temporary, and will pay off in the long run as I better learn how to find the "just-right" teaching point for each reader.

Confer with a "Text Under the Arm"

Once I started to become more practiced at conferring, I found this situation would happen to me. I would be sitting next to a student, working hard to listen and decide. Suddenly, the teaching point would become so clear. I would realize that I needed to help the student retell the main events of the chapter, and that maybe teaching the student to touch each page as she retold would be an appropriately supportive strategy. But then a wave of panic would sweep over me. If I would retell the student's chapter for her, I would have done her work! I would quickly think of a book that I might be able to use to demonstrate. Oh wait! It would be sitting over on the desk. Or was it by the easel? "I'll be right back, Rachel," I'd say, as I headed off searching, the student left expectantly waiting for my return.

Carl Anderson taught me the importance of being prepared for conferences with a text that I, and also the students, know well. This text may be the read-aloud or another lower-level chapter book with which my students are familiar. It may be the same text I've used in my minilesson demonstrations. The texts I choose are somewhat simplistic so that the student is able to concentrate on my thinking and application of a strategy, and not on the content of the book.

When teaching a student by demonstrating, I find it more helpful to teach him with my own demonstration text than with the student's book. This ensures a few things. First, it ensures that what I'm teaching is a generalizable strategy—that is, if I teach a strategy and show it in my book, then it has to be general enough that the student will be able to replicate it in his book. Sometimes, I find that if I merely teach by demonstrating in the student's book, I may end up teaching something that is so book-specific that I'm in essence teaching the book, not the reader. I want all of the strategies I teach to work in the student's book today and the book that the student will read tomorrow, and next month, and the following summer. Second, it allows the student to have ample opportunity to practice in his own book. If I demonstrate how to get an idea about a character in the student's book, he very likely ends up having the same idea that I do! There is no assurance that the student actually understood or applied the strategy because I did a lot of the work for him.

To get ready to use this text, I mark the book in many places (usually with different colored Post-it flags) and write on the flags the way that I plan to use them. Following is a short example from *Fox and His Friends,* by Edward

Excerpt from Fox and His Friends, by Edward Marshall

Transcribed Text	Teaching Point: Skill + *by* + Strategy	Think Aloud
"Fox, dear," said Fox's mom. "Just where do you think you are going?"	Identify the speaker of untagged dialogue *by* using context clues	"I notice here that the author didn't tell me who said this. I need to figure it out. I need to read the dialogue before and after and ask myself, "Who would have said that?"
"Out to have fun with the gang," said Fox.	Get an idea about a character *by* noticing the way a character talks to another character and asking yourself, "What kind of person would talk like that?"	"I can't believe Fox just talked that way to his mother! That's like talking back! I think that Fox is kind of a rude character."
"It's Saturday." "But today you must take care of little Louise," said Mom. "You're joking," said Fox. "I am *not* joking!" said Mom. And she gave Fox a look.	Understand character motivation *by* noticing cause and effect.	"I wonder why Fox finally took Louise. Let me reread what happened right before he did that. Oh, I bet it was because of the look his mother gave him."
"Come on, Louise," said Fox. Fox went to see his friend Dexter. But Dexter's mom came to the door. "Sorry, Fox," she said. "Dexter has to help at home all day." "That's no fun," said Fox. "Come on, Louise." Dexter watched from the window. "Sorry, Fox," he said.	Interpret the author's feelings or message *by* noticing patterns in a book and asking yourself, "What do these patterns tell me about how the author might feel about this subject?"	"I remember that Fox's mother gave Fox a job and Dexter's mother is giving Dexter a job. I wonder if the author thinks that mothers are always giving their kids jobs to do, and that's not very fun for kids."
Next Fox went to Betty's house. "Betty has chicken pox," said her mom. "Can she still play?" asked Fox.	Infer character traits *by* focusing on character action and asking yourself, "What kind of person would do that?"	"Betty has the chicken pox, but Fox still asks if she can play! He's not a very understanding character."
"Of course not," said Betty's mom. "Poor Betty," said Fox. "Come on, Louise" "Okay," said Louise. "Sorry, Fox," said Betty. "You can't help it," said Fox.	Revise thinking *by* looking for text evidence that does or doesn't fit with what you previously thought.	"Oh, before I thought that he wasn't very understanding but here he says, 'Poor Betty.' I guess he's a little bit understanding, but he still wants things his way."

Marshall. Here I have transcribed the text of the book in the left-hand column, the strategy and skill that I would teach with that part of the text in the center column, and an example of a think-aloud in the third column. This is one suggested template for how a book may serve multiple purposes, depending on what the student needs.

One of the many things that I love about yoga is that when you do it, it's called *practicing* yoga. By using that verb, there's an underlying assumption that I'm not expected to be perfect. Even though it is always challenging, I know that by learning all of the poses and the ways to practice, I'm progressing. What a wonderful way for me to look at my own conferring. Conferring is hard and takes practice. I can't expect myself to be perfect. On some days a conference or two will flop, just like on some days when I practice yoga my hamstrings are tight, my balance is off, and I fall to the ground while attempting a pose. But I know that with practice, planning, and preparation, my conferring will improve dramatically. (And my colleagues might even think it's magic!)

Classroom Applications

- Reflect on your own reading behaviors in order to get ideas for what to teach students. Pick a text and "spy" on yourself as you read it.
- Get to know the levels of the students in your class very well. Take a few books at each level and study them, asking yourself, "What skills does this level demand?" and plan for the things you might teach a student at that level.
- Put all of your note-taking and running records to good use. Use them to plan for what you might teach individual students. Having a game plan might help you feel more confident when you're first learning.
- Use your student assessments to look for patterns, to develop theories, and to craft long-term goals for individuals.
- Don't be afraid of reusing teaching demonstrations from past lessons! Repetition will help you to fine-tune your teaching and feel more equipped in a conference.
- Have a text that you and your students know (perhaps a past read-aloud) marked up with places where you could do an impromptu demonstration.
- Internalize a conferring structure. You may start by "boxing out" the parts of the conferences in the appendix, and then move to transcribing and analyzing your own conferences.

11

Working Efficiently: Group Conferring

Wilbur: "Congratulations! How many are there?"

Goose: "There are seven."

Charlotte: "Seven is a lucky number."

Goose: "Luck has nothing to do with it! It was good management and hard work."

— CHARLOTTE'S WEB (THE MOVIE)

In New York City public schools, it's not unusual to have between thirty and thirty-five students in an upper elementary classroom. When I started teaching third grade at P.S. 165 on Manhattan's Upper West Side in September 2001, I had thirty-three students enrolled in my class.

Every student in that class was truly an individual! I clearly remember Jasmine, the spunky tough girl who loved to read books like Paula Danziger's *Amber Brown* series. Jasmine had trouble staying focused in her reading, but she had such a knack for making connections and interpretations that went beyond the books she was reading and into the world. And I can't forget Luis. Luis was creative and artistic—he got a scholarship to attend a special performing-arts middle school to nurture his flute-playing talent. During reading workshop, he always looked so engaged in his books, but when I'd talk to him about what he was reading, he'd include more details from his imagination than from the actual text he was holding. And then there was Gregory, who had been stuck in level J for the past year and was determined to push himself into harder books this year. And Tiffani, who snuck in nonfiction even when we were in a whole-class character study because those were the books that spoke to her. I felt so overwhelmed by what each student needed until Amanda Hartman, my staff developer at the time and now a colleague of mine at the TCRWP, taught me the power of small-group strategy lessons.

Even though every student in the class was a unique individual, there were patterns across students. There were a few readers, like Gregory, who seemed stuck in lower-level books. There were a few readers, like Luis, who could benefit from strategies to help them be accountable to the text and retell with accuracy. And there were readers, like Jasmine, who read with such sophistication and would benefit from instruction that pushed their thinking. To use my conferring time more efficiently and effectively, I began doing more small group instruction—both planned and spontaneous—which allowed me to work with more of my students on a regular basis.

What Is a Small-Group Conference?

Small-group conferences occur when I pull a group of two to five readers together who need work with the same strategy. Small-group conferences have been described elsewhere as strategy lessons, because the focus for the group is on teaching a strategy, as opposed to teaching or introducing a specific book (Calkins 2001). Readers that come together in a small-group conference need not be reading the same book or even at the same level, although they may come together to practice a strategy on a shared text. This means that I may have a level-L reader who is holding James Howe's *Pinky and Rex,* a level-J reader who is holding Cynthia Rylant's *Poppleton in Spring,* and a level-Q reader who is holding Beverly Cleary's *Ramona Quimby, Age 8* in the same group conference. I might pull them together because I notice that all of them almost exclusively are retelling when they write about their reading, and I want to help them move toward writing more of their own original thinking. I might decide to teach them the strategy of noticing character interactions as a way to get ideas. I pull the group together, state my intention for the conference, demonstrate using a read-aloud they all are familiar with, and then have them practice the strategy in their own books. While they practice in their own books, I coach them along in their thinking. After about one or two minutes per student, I stop all of the students and repeat my teaching point, making clear that I expect them to continue what they just practiced independently in their own reading.

Figure 11-1.

Researching to Form Small Groups

I used to feel afraid of small-group conferences. My colleagues and I began to study our small-group work in reading workshop by first visiting each other's classrooms. In each of the classrooms, I noticed the teacher's methods were strong—they each did beautiful demonstrations, voicing-over their thinking as they read. But when they got to the part of the small-group conference where the students would try what was taught, it all became clear. What I noticed was that some readers needed the strategy, whereas others needed a similar strategy but not the one that just had been taught. I met with my colleagues later in the afternoon and we realized together that the problem wasn't doing a small-group conference; it was forming the small group with whom we'd work. Over the course of the next few weeks, we worked together to research ways that teachers predictably can pull together small groups of students who would benefit from learning the same strategy. The following ways tend to fall into two groups: ways to form small groups by analyzing data you already have, and ways to form spontaneous small groups by quick, targeted research.

Forming Groups Ahead of Time

Using Past Record-Keeping

In Chapter 12, I discuss some ways that you might consider developing a record-keeping system that works for you. It took me years to learn that, for my own record-keeping, it was important to record not only what I complimented and taught, but also other information about the reader. I found that when I pushed myself to do this, I often would write down several other potential teaching points for that student. Frequently, at the end of a conference, my notes look something like what is depicted in Figure 11-2.

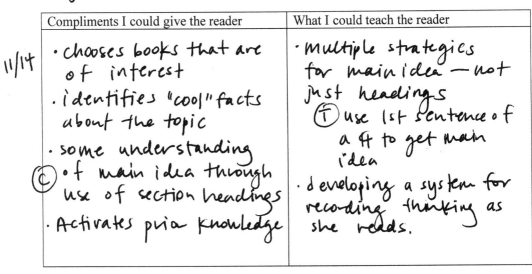

Figure 11-2.

You might notice from this example that I have listed many things that the student is doing well and many things that the student can use my help with to become a stronger reader. I've identified the *one* thing I complimented and the *one* thing I taught by marking them with a *C* in a circle or a *T* in a circle. So what happens, then, to all of the other stuff I jot down? I can always use that information to guide the research of my next individual conference, but I can also use it to help me form small groups.

About once a week, I try to sit down with my conferring note-taking binder and synthesize my notes. On a single sheet of paper, with the students' names running down one side and the goals for the class study running along the top, I try to determine which students might benefit from some follow-up instruction on certain skills and strategies. Figure 11-3 shows a completed form.

According to my key, I can see that there are a few students (Antony, Aidan, Deborah) who need follow-up instruction on getting the main idea of a section in their nonfiction books by using the first sentence of a section. There are eleven students who need work on getting ideas about their nonfiction books, so this most likely will become a string of a few minilessons that I teach to the whole class. I see five students (Alicia, Bobby, Haley, Samantha, William) who get stuck on challenging words and need to rely more on context clues, and so on. After fifteen minutes of work to synthesize my notes, I figured out what the next four small-group conferences could be in my classroom.

Using Running Records

Looking over your running records has the same benefit as looking over your conference notes. In Chapter 10, I write about how to analyze running records to determine the cueing systems that students use to make miscues as they read. I also can look at students' responses to literal and inferential questions, and any notes I may have jotted down about their fluency and intonation while reading. As I look across my students' running records, I look for patterns again. I might ask myself such questions as:

- Can I find a few readers who tend to only use the beginning letters of a word exclusively to try to figure it out?
- Can I find a few readers who need a lot of prompting in their retelling?

Non-Fiction Unit   November

	Understands Main Idea	Infers/ Has own ideas	Figures out Vocab using context clues	Synthesizes info. on the page	Makes connections btwn. texts
Antony	~	~			+
Alicia	+		*	~	
Aidan	~	~	+		
Belinda	*		*		*
Bobby		~	*		
Cadence	+	*		*	+
Christina		~			
Caleb			~	+	+
Dajuan		~	*		
Danielle	+	~			
Dayshawn		*		+	
Deborah	~				
Elizabeth	+	+	+		*
Gabrielle				+	
Hannah	+				
Haley			*		+
Jack		~			
Samantha			~		+
Tom	+		*		
Thea	+	~			
William			~	*	
Yolanda	+	~			
Zach			*	*	*

Key:
~ struggling
*developing, needs follow-up
+has demonstrated evidence

Figure 11-3. Conference notes synthesis.

- Can I find a few readers who have difficulty answering inference questions?
- Can I find a few readers who have difficulty reading fluently?
- Can I find a few readers who seem to ignore punctuation marks and read without expression or intonation?

I can sort my student's data into categories and plan out a series of small group conferences. Based on their retelling, printwork, fluency, intonation, and inference and interpretation, I might create a quick form (Figure 11-4) to help me to organize the analysis of my record-keeping.

Reading ending punctuation	Retelling	Inferring about Character	Using meaning
Melissa John Simone	Byron Jane	Cynthia Mehak Desiree Ramon	Jacob Phyllis Cynthia Ramon Melissa
Reading dialogue with expression	Reading fluently	Using syntax	
Melissa Simone	Melissa Jasmine Brant Toby	Jasmine Jane	

Figure 11-4. Sorting students into groups by skill.

Analyzing Student Artifacts

When my students are in the habit of jotting their thinking as they read and logging their books as they read them, these artifacts provide me with crucial data as I begin to sort them into groups. Once in a while, I ask my students to leave their notebooks and book logs on their desks as they go off to art class or lunch, and I move around the room with a clipboard, making notes as I go. As I look at their book logs, I might ask such questions as:

- Which students seem to be reading with lower volume than I expect?
- Which students have been reading the same level for a while?
- Which students aren't keeping up with their reading logs as I expect?
- Which students need to be reminded to keep up their reading of just-right chapter books even though we are also doing nonfiction reading?
- Which students are jumping around from topic to topic in nonfiction instead of sticking to one topic for a while?

As I sort through their reading notebooks, I look for evidence of my teaching from that unit of study. In a nonfiction unit, I may be looking to see:

- Which students are having trouble identifying main ideas?
- Which students are simply recalling facts instead of also having ideas?
- Which students are making notes of the new words they learn as they go, and which students don't seem to be using any vocabulary strategies?

I use one of the two forms introduced already—either a checklist or several boxes in which to collect students' names under categories—to organize my findings.

WAYS TO FORM SMALL GROUPS AHEAD OF TIME

- Try to write down more than just the teaching point from a conference, then sort this data to form small groups.
- After analyzing running records, look for trends across students.
- Use student artifacts from their reading (Post-its, notebooks) to look for trends.

Forming Groups Spontaneously

Conducting Quick Assessment

Sometimes I get so busy that I don't have time to sit down and sort through my conference notes or past running records to sort the students into small groups. Sometimes I find myself doing more on-the-go assessment and forming quick groups based on what I notice.

At any point in the reading workshop, I quickly can go around the room and observe student behaviors or do fast assessment of their reading based on the written records of their reading work in book logs, in reading notebooks, and on Post-its. When doing this kind of quick assessment, it's helpful for me to have a limited number of things in mind; otherwise I easily can get side-tracked into spending ten minutes or longer doing more in-depth analysis of one student's work.

To begin this quick assessment, I first create a few categories of antici-pated problems or concerns. For example, if I'm looking in September for observable behaviors of a second- or third-grade classroom, I might antici-pate that there are some readers who are pointing to words (which readers above a level E rarely need to do), readers who are reading aloud or mouthing words, readers who seem disengaged, or readers who are spend-ing more time writing than reading. I next divide a piece of paper into four boxes, find a good vantage point somewhere in the room, and just observe. Whenever I see someone who may need support in one of the categories, I just write the student's name in the appropriate box. Many students won't need these strategies in which case I would create a new category, and a few students will need more than one, so I write their names in all the places it belongs. As soon as I've spent a few minutes observing, I notice that I have around three to five names in one of those boxes. There's my group confer-ence! I don't delay—I promptly bring them to a large table or the meeting area and do a quick group conference.

Turning an Individual Conference into a Group Conference

There have been points in my reading workshop when I've felt like I should just tape-record myself and push play: I'd go from table to table, repeating the same conferences over and over to individual students. Eventually, it occurred to me to get into the habit of stopping myself a few minutes into individual conferences after I've decided on a teaching point. I pause and ask myself, "Does this seem like a conference that other students at the table might need?" If I have a hunch that the answer might be "yes," I quickly scan the table to see what the others are doing. If, in fact, some others could benefit from the conference, then I ask the others at the table to listen.

"Can I have all of your eyes and ears over here, please?" I say. "I'm going to help Angelica with something that I think will help all of you, too. Why don't you watch me show you, and then I'll help you all have a go at it." I then proceed with my demonstration and coach the whole table, not only Angelica.

Using Data Gleaned During Minilessons

After demonstrating a strategy to the whole class in the minilesson at the start of a workshop period, I always give the students a chance to have a quick try. This quick try might mean that they talk to their partners for a minute, or that they jot something down. This active involvement time is an invaluable resource of information.

When students turn and talk, they all are set up to practice the same strategy, often from the same text. When I set them up to try out the strategy, I often say something like, "So now that you all saw me try to figure out the main idea of this section by rereading the first and last sentences on the page, I want you to try it. I have another page from this same book on the overhead. With your partner, would you read this section, and then reread the first and last sentences? See if you can figure out what this page is mostly about and how you knew." While the students are turning and talking to practice the strategy, I move around among them, jotting notes. I listen carefully, asking myself questions such as: Which readers simply are stating details, not the main idea? Which readers simply are reading the sentence and are struggling with putting it in their own words? As I listen, I note the students who are having difficulties, knowing I can ask them to join me immediately after the minilesson as I help them to apply the strategy in their own reading.

Being able to listen to many students quickly during a brief one- to two-minute turn-and-talk takes some finesse. An easier way to get at the same goal is to give each student a small slip of paper or Post-it note at the start of the lesson. During the active involvement, I ask the students to jot down what they otherwise would have spoken to a partner. I then ask them to pass the papers forward or leave them right on their rug spots. After they have settled into their own independent reading, I take the papers and sort them into piles, and those piles become my small groups.

Either of these ways seems a bit easier to me than looking at the students' own writing about their independent reading, simply because in a minilesson all the students are writing about the same text that I'm familiar with, whereas in their independent reading they're in different texts. Their responses and thinking will usually fall into clearer categories after a minilesson. The drawback to this kind of research is that how a student fares with practicing the strategy during the minilesson on a shared, familiar text that is often read aloud to her isn't always predictive of how the student applies the strategy to her own independent reading. For this reason, it's important that data gleaned from a minilesson is not the only data I use to assess the readers.

FORMING SPONTANEOUS SMALL GROUPS

- ■ Determine a few predictable problems that are easily observable and scan the room, quickly moving from student to student looking only for those few things.
- ■ After researching one student's reading, stop and ask yourself, "Could anyone else use this strategy?" If so, call the rest of the table's attention and demonstrate and coach them all.
- ■ Give students a chance to have a quick try with the strategy during the minilesson. Have the students write what they're thinking on Post-its, and collect and sort the Post-its into small groups.
- ■ Listen during the students' chance to practice a strategy during a minilesson, quickly move among them while taking notes, and sort them into categories based on the level of support they need.

Structure and Methods of Group Conferring

You've learned so far in this section that the research in a group conference happens either well in advance or right before you form the group. Therefore, when you start off the group conference, you can begin by just telling the students why you've called the meeting. Clearly state to them what you noticed, and the one teaching point that you're going to introduce to them to help make them stronger readers.

The next part of the conference happens just like an individual conference. I can do shared reading, demonstration, or explanation and example. I am likely to make my decision of what method to use based on the level of support I hope to give the readers in the group (see Chapter 6 for more information).

From there, I want to get all of the students actively working right away. This is a common pitfall—it shouldn't be that as I begin to coach one reader, the rest just sit and wait for me. They may practice the strategy in their own independent reading books or on an independent-level text that I prepare ahead of time. I move between each student, coaching when necessary. There may come a time when a student does something so amazing that I want the rest of the group to watch—in this instance, I may stop all of the students and ask them to watch one reader before returning to their own practicing.

Once students have had some time to practice with support from me, I send them back to their own independent reading, encouraging them to continue to practice the strategy. I take notes on what I taught and what I observed when they tried the strategy, and these notes often help me plan my next individual or small-group conference!

For some children, small-group conferences may be best used when in a string of meetings with the teacher to work on one strategy over the course of a week in different texts. Take, for example, a small group of students who are working on reading with intonation that matches the character's feeling. It could be that during the first group conference, the teacher demonstrates the strategy and spends one or two minutes coaching each reader in his own book. It is likely, though, that the students could still use some follow-up. In this instance, the teacher could decide to coach the group again the following day and begin simply by restating the teaching point and encouraging them to get started. This small group would take less time than the day before and the students will get valuable follow-up instruction. Consider, then, that sometimes the small-group conferences are not just a one-shot deal, but instead could be a sequence of coaching opportunities with a small group over time.

Balancing Small-Group and Individual Conferences

Sometimes when teachers learn how to do group conferences, they say, "This is great! It's so efficient! I can see so many more students! I should do this all the time!" While the temptation is certainly there, I recommend trying to maintain a balance of individual and group conferences for a couple of reasons. One, my individual time is crucial to doing in-depth assessment with one reader. I might notice that in a group conference, there isn't much research except for what I notice once the students started practicing the strategy I taught. Compare this to the amount of data that I glean from working with one student. Look, for example, at the notes from only one conference with Angelica that are at the beginning of this chapter. Another reason is that if I see my students in many small groups, I start seeing them almost every other day. While at first this may sound enticing, students need time to practice the strategies that I've taught them. If they're always given more instruction, they'll become swamped with many strategies when they should really be practicing a few skills at a time with more depth.

Classroom Applications

- Put to use all of those notes that you spend so much time taking! Mine your conference notes and running records for trends across your class. Sort students into groups based on a few categories that are aligned with your goals.

- When you spend time checking in on your students' written artifacts (such as book logs, reading notebooks, and Post-it notes), you also might consider sorting them into categories based on what you notice. A small amount of time doing this sort of assessment will help you plan a week's worth of small groups.

- Keep a few categories in mind when doing quick assessment in the midst of reading workshop to form small groups. Having more focus will help you to see evidence more quickly.

- Try to stick to a predictable structure with your group conferences, just as you would with minilessons or individual conferences. This structure will help your groups to run smoothly and will keep you on a schedule.

- Consider that, at times, your small-group conference can be done as a string of lessons where you coach a group of students to practice one strategy over a week or two.

- Be sure to have a plan for how you'll balance small-group and individual time. Keep in mind that small-group conferences take longer, about eight to ten minutes, so plan to do only one or two per workshop period to allow some time to see individual students.

12 Keeping Records

> " 'What an amazing day!' Mrs. Martinez said. 'Who would believe it? If only someone had written it all down.' "
>
> — NOTHING EVER HAPPENS ON 90TH STREET, BY RONI SCHOTTER

Why Take Notes?

I used to dismiss record-keeping. "I know my students really well. I don't need to write anything down," I'd say, or, "Taking notes means I can't listen well." But then I experienced some embarrassing moments that were the result of not writing things down, like the time I finally sat down with Pablo after what must have been a month to discover he'd been sitting with the same book that whole time. I didn't know it had been so long because I had no system for writing down when I conferred with each student. Or there's the time I had a parent-teacher conference with Melissa's mother and was caught unable to recall specific details about the strategies I'd taught her across the year. And those are just two examples. It's often the quiet ones, the ones who look engaged and independent, whom I lose track of in my workshop. Even those of us least in need of gingko biloba extract still have memory failure from time to time.

Developing my own system for recording and keeping track of both individual and whole-class assessment data is crucial to doing reading conferences well. Conference notes make my analysis of student-reading processes much more on target, ensure that I have an equitable system for seeing all the students in my class, help hold students accountable for past teaching, and help me feel prepared and informed when speaking to parents, support personnel, and administration.

Discovering a System and Routine That Works

Throughout my years as a teacher, I've been through about a half dozen different record-keeping forms. I now realize that the exact forms that I used for record-keeping weren't as important as making sure I used something. I ended up with a system for recording data about individual students as well as a system to record information for my class as a whole. Because I had my readers often grouped in partnerships and clubs, I also needed to decide on a system for recording what I noticed about students in those social groupings.

In addition to developing the forms I use, I had to figure out when and how I'd use them. When I first started conferring, it took everything I had to listen carefully and intently to a student to try to figure out a compliment and teaching point, to have my materials ready to teach her, and to coach her while trying it. Juggling record-keeping as well would have been too much for me to handle. So I developed a routine: After I had finished a conference, I stayed by the student and jotted some notes before getting up and making my way to a new student. There's a benefit to this—by sticking around, I sometimes find that I need to coach a little more or give an extra reminder, and having me physically there also helps to hold the student accountable. After years of practice conferring—when I felt more prepared in the conferences because I'd taught the same ones over and over, and the structure of a conference was internalized—I became able to listen to a student and jot notes at the same time. The benefit to this, of course, is speed. I'm now able to confer with many more students each day.

Individual Record-Keeping

The system I always find most helpful for recording my conferences is a simple two-sided form that I adapted from Carl Anderson, a widely regarded guru of conferring in the writing workshop, and author of *Assessing Writers* (2005) and *How's it going?* (2000). This is the form that is used throughout this book.

On one side, I record potential compliments and on the other side potential teaching points. I make several copies of this form and place these copies in a three-ring binder. Each student has his own section where I keep this individual record-keeping form. At the start of a conference, I quickly can turn to the student's section, skim over past notes, and begin a conference looking for evidence of past teaching—either by observing or by asking questions. This routine, I find, helps to hold students accountable and helps to hold me accountable.

I also make it a habit that, on this form, I write down more than just the compliment and teaching point from the conference. I see every conference as an assessment opportunity, so I try to push myself to write down several strengths that I see evidence of as well as several areas that the student needs support in. Because I have this extra data, I can more easily form small groups and I often can begin a new conference by checking up on past observations, thereby giving me a lens for studying that student (Figure 12-1). In each student's section, I also keep a collection of running records that I've done with that student. These forms provide important data for analyzing miscues and for doing conferences based on printwork and fluency.

Whole-Class Record-Keeping

In addition to having data about individual students, it's also helpful to have pages of record-keeping where I can see my class at a glance. I have a form, probably at the front of my binder, where I can glance quickly at student's reading levels. I also have a form where I can see the dates that I met with each student in my class. Finally, I may want to have some forms where I can look across a set of reading skills or unit goals to help me form small groups based on what I've observed.

To ensure that I'm conferring with students equitably, it's important that I record the date of a conference on a single page each time I sit down with a student. I say equitably because it is very likely that I'd see the one-third of my class who are most struggling about twice as often as I'd see the two-thirds of the class who are reading at or above grade level. This is often because I want to support the more struggling students through a series of conferences with leaner and leaner coaching as they move toward independence. I mark their

Mihak

Compliments I could give the reader	What I could teach the reader
4/18 · envisioning the scene — characters ? setting · good sense of char.'s mood ⓒ · has many post-its, mostly retelling	· to jot ideas, not just retelling by using one ⓣ of char. inference strategies (reminded her of 3...) · envision ch. emotion
4/25 ⓒ · post·its more diverse & now—some retell, some char. traits [ready to start new book in series —] · understands change that happened to the character, ? how the character dealt w/ it.	· how to get ready for new book — review what ⓣ you know about the char. + make a prediction · interpretation - what's the story really about

Figure 12-1.

Conference Record	

Teacher Name: Serravallo   Grade: 3

Name	Dates
Edward *	(J) 1/3 1/5
Meridith	(N) 1/4
Jessica *	(L) 1/5 1/10
Frank B	(M) 1/4
Gregory	(O) 1/3 1/10
Mihak	(Q) 1/5
Desiree	(O) 1/5
Byron	(P) 1/5
Celeste	(M) 1/6
Anibal *	(K) 1/3
Henry	(N) 1/4
Alex	(M) 1/7
Simone *	(L) 1/3 1/10
Hong *	(J) 1/7
Syeed	(O) 1/4
August	(Q) 1/7
Tiffany *	(I) 1/6 1/10
Jamel *	(L) 1/3 1/6
Kamara	(M) 1/7
Frank G *	(J) 1/4 1/7
Renee	(O) 1/6
Tyrell	(P) 1/4
Dorian	(N) 1/6

Figure 12-2. One way to keep track of who I meet with in a conference.

names with a star so that, at a glance, I can be sure that I am working with them more but still giving them planty of independent time. Such a form is shown in Figure 12-2.

I've also found it helpful to have a sheet where I can see my class reading levels, partnerships, and book clubs at a glance. I use this form not only as an at-a-glance sheet in my own note-taking binder, but also as a way to communicate with parents during parent-teacher conferences. To do this, I simply mask the other students' names to show parents where their students' reading levels lie in relation to the rest of the class (Figure 12-3).

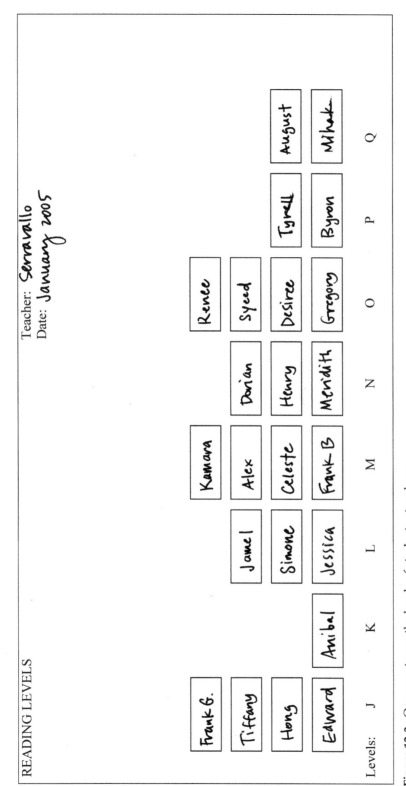

READING LEVELS

Teacher: Serravallo
Date: January 2005

Frank G.							Renee	
Tiffany		Jamel	Kamara	Dorian	Syeed			August
Hong		Simone	Alex	Henry	Desiree	Tyrell		
Edward	Anibal	Jessica	Celeste	Frank B	Meridith	Gregory	Byron	Mihok

Levels: J   K   L   M   N   O   P   Q

Figure 12-3. One way to see the levels of students at a glance.

Figure 12-4.

Checklists are very effective to see, at a glance, what most of the students in my room are doing securely and what readers need more support with. When I have time, I go through my individual conference notes and, using a coding system (with + for "has shown evidence," a * for "developing," and ~ for "struggling"), I synthesize a month's worth of note-taking onto one page. I use that to inform future teaching (see Figure 11-3). Sometimes, I take five or ten minutes out of my conferring time to do some research in the room. I go around the classroom with a few goals in mind and check each student's written records of her thinking (like Post-its and notebooks) for evidence of these goals. I mark off on a one-page checklist my reactions to what I see. These checklists also come in handy for recording data during read-aloud conversations and what I notice the readers doing during the active involvement part of minilessons. All of these class-at-a-glance forms have their own section in my reading note-taking binder.

Keeping Records on Partnerships and Clubs

Book clubs and partnerships, described in more detail in Chapter 9, are opportunities for readers to have social experiences over their books. Students might discuss ideas they were having as they read alone, revisit ideas that the group had talked about in a previous meeting, sit side by side and read aloud together, or even act out parts of the book. Before I begin to confer with these groups and pairs, I find it helpful to think through the ways that I record what I notice and what I teach.

Figure 12-5 shows an example of a form that I use for partnerships (the club form looks the same except in the first column, which says "club members' names"). You may notice that I have the students' names typed into the form. This is because the partnerships remain stable for a while in my classroom, and by having the names pretyped into the boxes I easily can see at a glance whom I still need to meet with.

Keeping Records on Group Conferences

Note-taking for group conferences was always a struggle for me because many of my small-group conferences were impromptu. I recently learned from Lauren Boneville, at P.S. 68 in Queens, New York, a wonderful way to manage it. Lauren has a single page with a box for each student. When she does a group conference, she records the date and teaching point in one student from the group's box, and then simply writes "see [student's name]" in the other two or three boxes of students from the group. She also may take some notes on how well the student is able to use the strategy independently after trying the strategy in the group. An example of this form is shown in Figure 12-6. To make it even simpler, I use the coding system I use in my checklist to synthesize notes. Having a class grid like this also allows me to see, at a glance, whom I still need to meet with and helps me to avoid teaching one reader in many small groups during one week. As tempting as it is to pull my most struggling readers into every group, those students also need to have plenty of time to practice one new strategy without being overwhelmed with many new ones to try.

Figure Out How You'll Choreograph It All

It is helpful for me to think through some of the choreography of conferring. Specifically, how will I ensure I teach readers equitably?

I find it helpful to have some sense of whom I'll be meeting with each day. Some years, I make a schedule for myself so that I can be sure to see my class equitably, remembering that students who are reading below grade level probably should be seen with more frequency. Because issues always come up and it's helpful to be flexible, teachers who have schedules often have a few

Partnership Conferences Unit of Study: Character			
Partner's Names & Date	Compliment	Teaching Point	Next steps
Edward and Byron 10/12	Good eye contact	Respond to what partner said before stating own idea	Follow-up on T. P.
Meridith and Melissa			
John and Sydney 10/15	Nice job talking for a while about one idea	Play "Devil's Advocate" → disagreeing can grow new ideas + spice up convers.	Follow-up on T. P.
Elizabeth and Joseph 10/12	Good conversation comes from stating ideas, not only retelling	When stating ideas, use evidence from the text	When referencing text, make sure everyone turns to that page
Mihak and Alex 10/15	Very prepared for conversation	State ideas + evidence, then discuss.	During indiv. conf I make sure post-its have more original thinking
Renee and Tiffany			
Frank B and Tyrell 10/2	Good retelling	Once you've agreed on the story (retellings accurate) move to stating ideas → "I think..."	During indiv. conferences — strategies for getting ideas about char.

Figure 12-5. Partnership conferences form.

Group Conferring Notes — Week of **10/25**

Antony (+) TP: study char. by noticing when they are abs. from scene	Alicia	Aidan	Belinda (+) TP: study char. by asking "why did you do that?"	Bobby
Cadence	Christina	Caleb (+) see Antony	Dajuan	Danielle (~) TP: study character by analyzing interactions
Dayshawn	Deborah (+) see Belinda	Elizabeth	Gabrielle (+) see Antony	Hannah (+) see Danielle
Haley (~) See Antony	Jack (+) See Danielle	Samantha	Tom (*) See Belinda	Thea
William (*) See Belinda	Yolanda	Zach (*) See Danielle		

Key:
~ struggling
*developing, needs follow-up
+has demonstrated evidence

Figure 12-6.

"must-see" students on their schedules, and a few "open" slots. One year, I allowed students to sign up for their own conferences. I caution against this only because I have found that students sometimes are less accountable for their work if they know for sure that the teacher won't be coming around to see them for a few more days. This isn't true in all classrooms, though, so it's up to each teacher to make that determination for herself. I also have to decide whether I want to make the conferring schedule public or private to the class. Here is a sample for how one third-grade teacher broke up her fifty minutes of reading workshop (remember that, minus the minilesson and share time, she had about thirty-five minutes of independent-reading time each day in which to do book clubs or partnership talk, individual conferences, and group conferences).

	Monday	Tuesday	Wednesday	Thursday	Friday
Talk time (clubs/partners)	5 min—goal setting/plans		10 min (8 students)		10 min (8 students)
Group conferences	10 min (4 students)	15 min (4 students)	10 min (4 students)	15 min (4 students)	10 min (4 students)
Individual conferences	20 min (3 students)	20 min (4 students)	15 min (3 students)	20 min (4 students)	15 min (3 students)
Totals	7 students	11 students	15 students	11 students	15 students

In this example, there is a total of fifty-nine students that she works with across the week in some fashion. Even with a large class of thirty students or so, she still is able to work with almost every student twice.

Classroom Applications

■ Plan a record-keeping system. Plan to have records that track individual progress across time, as well as whole-class at-a-glance records. Don't forget that you also want to keep track of students' reading levels and the dates that you see them in conferences.

■ Consider planning out how you'll work with each student in your class equitably—ensuring that no student goes a week without a conference of some kind.

Conference Transcripts

Moving a Student to a New Level

Method: Explanation and Example

Teacher: So, Shanique, I see you've chosen a few *Judy Moody* books in order to try out this new level. And I also see that you've kept some of your favorite series—*Fox and Friends.* Good. You've got some of each in your baggie of books. I want to give you a compliment.

Shanique: Uh-huh.

Teacher: I like how you've chosen a few *Judy Moody* books. That's a really smart thing to do when you're moving to a new level. You know so much already from reading a bunch of books from the same series—these *Fox* books by James Marshall—and now when you get to this new level, you can use what you know from one book in the series to help you with the next book, and the next book, and the next book. It's smart to pick a bunch of books from the same series when you move to a new level.

The teacher gave a compliment that reinforced a strategy.

Teacher: I can't wait for you to get started in this new series because I think you're really going to like these characters—Judy and her little brother Stink! Before you get started, though, I wanted to give you a little tip that might help you feel like this new level is just right for you. You know how in *Fox and Friends* there are only a few characters you needed to keep track of? There's Fox and his little sister, his mother, and a few friends? Well, once you get to this new level, you're going to come across a lot of characters right away. So one of the things that I like to do is to keep track of the characters by jotting a list of their names and something about them on a Post-it or in my notebook, and then I can refer back to it when I get confused. Remember during read-aloud how we were doing this together for *Because of Winn-Dixie?* Let's look together at that chart we started. Remember how we charted the names and who they were?

The teacher gave an example from previous teaching in the read-aloud.

Shanique: Yeah. I see we put the characters' names. There are a lot of characters in this book! We wrote down something about each one, like how each character looks and who the character is related to.

Teacher: You got it. Why don't you try this strategy out in your book? Read the first few pages of your book and take this Post-it to jot down the names of the characters who are introduced. Remember to ask yourself, "How is this character related to the main character?" Or, "What can I write down so I can remember who this person is?"

Shanique: [takes a few minutes and writes] Stink = Judy's brother. He's annoying to her. She wants him to leave her alone.

Teacher: Shanique—good job identifying a new character. Take a peek at the class chart again. What do you notice that's different between the class chart and yours?

The teacher coached the reader to use the strategy.

Shanique: Uh, you didn't write as much as me.

Teacher: Yeah. You don't need to retell the scene. Just jot something to help you remember. What words do you think you really need to help you remember?

Shanique: Um, just that Stink is Judy's brother.

Teacher: Okay. You don't have to erase this, but for the next character, just jot down a quick note, okay?

Shanique: [continues and jots down] Rocky—Judy's best friend.

Teacher: "Nice, Shanique. Keep up the good work of jotting down just the character's name and a quick reminder of how they are related to the main character, or a note to help you remember who they are. I'll check back in with you soon to see how this book is working out for you!

The teacher restated the strategy in a way that lets the reader know it will help her in all books with multiple characters.

Supporting Students During Whole-Class Studies

Method: Demonstration

Teacher: Hi, Ramon. How's your reading going today?

Ramon: It's going good. I'm reading this book, *Horrible Harry Goes to the Moon*.

Teacher: That Harry is something else, isn't he? What a character. So what part of the book are you up to?

Ramon: Well, I just started it today, so I'm only up to this part. [Ramon points to page 4.]

Teacher: Can you tell me about what you've read so far?

The teacher researches the reader by having a conversation about his book.

Ramon: Well, these kids are fighting about sitting, so Doug made sitting a job. Sid keeps pushing . . . um . . . um . . . I forget her name. Sid keeps on pushing her, and he thinks of an idea, and they want to make sitting down a job.

Teacher: I'm a little confused. What do you mean when you said he makes sitting a job?

Ramon: Well, there's this couch, and everyone wants to sit on it instead of sitting on the rug, and so one of the kids says that sitting can be a job and everyone can get a turn.

Teacher: Ah, I see. So what are you thinking about as you're reading, Ramon?

The teacher begins to research the reader's higher-level thinking after checking his literal understanding.

Ramon: I'm thinking that the teacher will have a big surprise for the whole class.

Teacher: Ah, so you're making a prediction about what's going to happen in the story.

Ramon: Yeah, 'cuz that happened in another *Horrible Harry* book.

Teacher: Are you thinking about the characters at all?

The teacher keeps researching the reader to figure out what other strategies she can support him with.

Ramon: Yeah, I'm thinking that Sid is a mean character because he's pushing people in his class. And I'm thinking that Doug is a helpful character because he's coming up with an idea to help.

Teacher: Ramon, you're doing so many smart things today in your reading. You're thinking about what you know from other books in the series to help you understand this one. You're also using things that the characters do in the book to get an idea about them. This is important to do because, as a reader of fiction, we don't just follow the plot of the story, but we also follow the ideas that we have about our characters. This is something you should always do when you're reading fiction.

The teacher gave a compliment that named specifically what the reader is doing well and why he should keep doing it.

Teacher: So let's work a little more on building ideas about the characters. Today, I want to teach you that characters, like real people, are complex. That means that there is more to them than just one character trait. Like, today I might be grumpy because I didn't get enough sleep last night. But later today, I might be telling jokes to my friends at dinner, and they might think I'm a funny person. One person can be both grumpy and funny. I wonder if you're going to find the same thing to be true in your book. I wonder if, as you're reading, you're going to find out new things about this "mean" Sid or this "helpful" Doug that will make you get to know them a little better as a character and as a person who is not just one way.

Watch me as I try to get more than one idea about a character in my book. Right here, Fox is bossing his sister around, and I got the idea that he is pushy and bossy. He also bosses his friends around on the next page, here. That's more support for my idea. But here, where he loses the race and crashes into a flower bed, I was thinking that he's a little bit rude and selfish. He doesn't apologize and he ruined his neighbor's flowers! So Ramon, I'm thinking that Fox has quite a few characteristics that make him a somewhat unpleasant character. He's both bossy, rude, and selfish. Did you see how I read on, noticing more things that Fox did, and I tried to come up with many words to describe the kind of character he is?

Ramon: Yes.

Teacher: Let's have you try this now with your book. Read on a little bit and pay attention to things your characters do, and try to get more ideas about them.

The teacher prompts the reader to try the strategy in his own book after he observes the teacher's demonstration.

Ramon: [reads silently] Well, here Harry is talking, and he says "once in a blue moon," and nobody but him knows what that is.

Teacher: So what does that tell you about the kind of character he is?

Ramon: Maybe he's smart. But also, he kind of brags about it.

Teacher: I think you might be onto something there. So something the character said helped you get an idea about him. Whenever you come to a part when the character acts, says, or thinks something, you can think, "What kind of a character would do that?" and see if you can add more words to how you describe the character. That will help you get to know the character really well, just like you get to know real people. I know you're just in the beginning of your book, so I want you to start collecting all of these ideas about the character, and we'll talk again soon about how all of these ideas will help you grow a bigger theory about him. It will help you to primarily pay attention to just one character, maybe Harry since he's the main character of the book.

Ramon: Okay.

The teacher ended this conference by explaining the strategy step by step and tucking in tips for the reader, such as focusing on one main character.

Following Up on a Previously Taught Skill

Method: Demonstration

Teacher: Hi, Ramon. I see you're sticking with these *Horrible Harry* books.

Ramon: Yeah, I finished the other one about the moon, and now I'm reading this one, *Horrible Harry and the Ant Invasion.*

Teacher: When we last talked, you were working on getting ideas about the character in your books. We talked about how you can notice things that the character does as well as the way he speaks. Can you show me some places in the last book where you continued to try that after the conference?

The teacher began by researching the previously taught strategy.

Ramon: Here, on page 18, I wrote a Post-it that says I think Sid is funny because he's telling jokes. And here on page 24, Sid says, "Mary's right, Harry's wrong. Case closed." And I had the idea that he is a little bit mean. And here on page 40, it says that Harry bragged. So I wrote down that he's a bragging character.

Teacher: Great. I like how you put the Post-its on the pages where you had the idea, so when you went back to talk about it, you could tell me your idea and you could talk about what in the text gave you that idea. Readers not only have ideas about their books, but they also provide evidence, or proof, from the text. You did that here and you also did that the last time we talked. So keep that up.

The teacher gave a compliment that reinforced a strategy she noticed the reader using in the past conference as well as in the current one.

Teacher: Do you have any ideas about the characters in this new *Horrible Harry* book?

Ramon: Yeah. In this book, I put a Post-it here that said Harry is smart at science because he knows a lot about ants. And here I wrote a Post-it that says that Harry is smart because he got the ants to come back.

Teacher: You're doing some good work in this book, too, Ramon. I think that it's wise that you're paying close attention to Harry, the main character. He is a character who is going to show up on just about every page in the book and that will give you lots of opportunities to have ideas about him as a character. Now, since you've read several *Horrible Harry* books and Harry is a character in all of these books, I thought you could start to put all of your ideas together and form a big theory about him as a character. This is a little bit more than just letting one part give you an idea. When you build a theory about a character, you put together all the different ideas that you have about the character by noticing patterns in the way the character acts.

The teacher not only stated the teaching point, but also explained it in detail. Next, she demonstrates the teaching point in her own book.

Teacher: So let me show you what I mean by telling you a little about the theory that I have about the character, Fox, in the book *Fox and Friends.* I'm going to start by looking across my Post-its, then I'm going to tell you what my theory is based on the pattern I see. Finally, I'll retell the main events of the story in a way that makes sense to someone who hasn't read the book before—you. Here's a Post-it that says, "Fox talks back to his mother. That's rude." And here's a Post-it that says, "Fox is selfish." And here's a Post-it that says, "Fox is bossy." Hmm. Okay, let me think. How can I put these ideas together to make a bigger theory? Well, I think my theory about Fox is that he's a character who is mostly selfish. He wants people to do what he wants, when he wants it.

Okay, now let me retell the parts of the story that go with my theory so that it makes sense to someone who hasn't read it before. In the beginning of the story, Fox's mother asks him to take care of Louise, and he talks back to her. This shows that he's kind of selfish because he doesn't want to help out his mother. And then, when he goes to each of his friends' houses and finds out that they can't play because they have to help out at home or because they are sick with the chicken pox, he gets upset. This also shows that he's selfish because he doesn't understand that other people have things they need to do. And at the end of this chapter, when he goes to the park with his sister and she goes missing, he seems like he's more worried about getting in trouble for losing her than about actually losing her. Then he bribes her by buying her ice cream. That's selfish, too.

So Ramon, did you see how I put my ideas together to make one theory, and then I retold the parts of the story so that it supports my thinking and makes sense to someone who hasn't read the book before? I want you to try it with Harry.

Ramon: [takes a few moments to read back over his Post-its from this book and the other book]

The teacher takes a minute to record some notes about the reader as he's thinking.

Ramon: Okay, well, in the moon book, I wrote that Harry was smart because he uses big words and knows a lot of facts about the moon. And in the ant book, I wrote that he is smart because he figured out how to get the ants back. So my theory about Harry is that he's smart. But in a couple of places, he also kind of brags about himself. So I think he's smart and he knows it.

Teacher: Nice! You used all of your Post-its and put them together to come up with a theory. So now you can try to retell the parts of the book that support your theory.

Ramon: The character of Harry is smart because he knows a lot of moon facts. And in this book . . .

Teacher: Hold on, Ramon. You need to give me a little more in your retelling. Remember, tell it like I've never read the book.

As soon as the teacher recognized that the reader needed a little more support, she stepped in to coach him.

Ramon: Okay, in this book, the class is learning about the moon and their teacher gets a telescope. And Harry knows a lot about the moon and shows off what he knows in the classroom and outside when they're looking at the moon through the telescope. And this shows he's smart but kind of a show-off, too.

Teacher: That was much better. Try to do the same thing in this next book.

The teacher asks the reader to try the new strategy in more than one place so she can make sure he is ready to do this on his own when she leaves.

Ramon: Okay, in this book [touches *Horrible Harry and the Ant Invasion*] the class is learning about ants. The teacher orders ants in the mail and Harry wants to be in charge of taking care of them. Then some ants escape, and Harry said it's his job to find them, so he get the ants back by putting peanut butter on his finger. I think that was smart of him to put peanut butter on his finger. He knows what ants like.

Teacher: Ramon, you've done great work here in these books. The way that you continued to use the strategy of getting ideas based on things the characters do and say, and how you have evidence for your ideas. What you just learned today is that you can also look across your thinking in a book to get a big theory about a character. And when you talk about the theory and retell parts of the book, you need to retell in a way that makes sense to someone who doesn't know the story. I want you to remember this. Later when you meet with your reading partner, you can tell him about your theory and make sure that you're retelling like you just practiced with me.

Ramon: Okay.

Teacher: Great work, Ramon. I'm really proud of you.

Improving Student Conversations About Books

Method: Proficient Partner
In this conference, a group of students are meeting in a book club.

Molly: Okay, well, I was having the idea that the character Baseball Ballerina is kind of like the character Oliver Button.

James: Can you say more about that?

Molly: Yeah. They both dance on a stage in the story, so that's why I think that they're alike.

Juantrice: I agree with you, Molly. They both have to dance on the stage. And I think they're also both kind of nervous about it.

James: Yeah, Baseball Ballerina is afraid that people are going to think she's a wimp. She wants to play baseball, not dance. And Oliver Button, he wants to dance, not play sports.

Molly: So are you saying that they're the same because they're scared?

James and Juantrice: Yeah.

James: Christina, what do you think?

Christina: Well, I was thinking about the parents in the two stories. And I'm thinking they're kind of alike, too. Like, Baseball Ballerina's mom is kind of pushy because she makes her daughter wear pink even though she doesn't want to. And Oliver Button's dad isn't too happy that he wants to dance instead of play ball.

The teacher sits down in the circle with the readers and acts like a fellow book club member.

Teacher: Hmm. So I'm thinking about stereotypes here. What is it that the author wants us to think about what boys *should* do and what girls *should* do?

James: I think that the author's saying that you don't have to listen to your parents.

Molly: No! That's not what the author's saying. Sorry, James, but I disagree.

James: So what do you think it is, then?

Molly: I think the author is saying that you don't have to do something just because it's what people think you should do. Like, it's okay to be an individual.

Juantrice: I agree with Molly. Oliver Button is an individual and, in the end, the kids end up crossing out the word "sissy" and putting "star." I think that part shows that if you're an individual, people will accept you, maybe.

Teacher: Hmm. And I'm thinking about the stereotype of the parents, too . . .

The teacher got the other readers started with an idea and let them discuss it with their own opinions.

Christina: Yeah, that's what I was thinking about. Like, the parents just want what they think is best for their kids.

James: Yeah, I think they're afraid they'll get teased if they don't do what's expected.

Juantrice: But what's weird about that is that Baseball Ballerina is worried of the *opposite.* She's worried that if she does stuff that others think is girly—like wear pink—she'll get teased.

Christina: Maybe it's okay for girls to do stuff that some people think is boy stuff, but not okay for boys to do stuff that some people think is girl stuff.

At this point the teacher steps out of her book-club-member role and speaks to the readers as the teacher. She names the strategy so readers can replicate it without her.

Teacher: I'm so impressed with how you're all thinking. Let me name what we were doing just now to help us get more ideas. We're thinking about *stereotypes.* We're thinking about what the author is showing us about what some people think about certain people, and we're allowing that to help us get ideas. Keep going without me. Nice work.

Following Up on a Previously Taught Skill

Method: Shared Reading
This conference starts with the teacher reminding the reader about the strategy she learned in a previous conference and by researching how the student is doing with the strategy.

Teacher: Theresa, the last time we were together I taught you how to pay attention to the character's feelings. Can you show me a place in your book where you jotted down the character's feelings?

Theresa: On page 6 of *Minnie and Moo Go Dancing,* I wrote down the word "relaxed" because I thought Minnie was relaxed when she watched the sunset with Moo.

Teacher: Great work Theresa. I am glad you are remembering to pay attention to the character's feelings and jot them on a Post-it note. Can you please read me page 6 from your book?

Theresa: [begins reading accurately, but in a monotone voice]

At this point the teacher decides on a teaching point and begins explaining it to the reader.

Teacher: Okay, Theresa. You can stop reading. I am thinking you are ready to learn a new strategy today. I want to teach you how you can use the character's feelings to read with more expression. You can make your voice match the character's feelings. For example, if the character is sad, your voice can sound sad, and if your character is excited, your voice can sound excited. Let's practice this on a page from our read-aloud. This is a page from *Poppleton Has Fun.* It is the page where Poppleton is asking Cherry-Sue if she wants to go to the movies with him. Do you remember that part?

Theresa: [nods]

Teacher: Theresa, I would like you to listen and pay attention to the way I change my voice when someone is talking to try and sound like the character. In this case, I am going to make my voice sound like Cherry-Sue. [reads a few lines with lots of expression]

Theresa: [follows along as the teacher reads]

After demonstrating the new strategy for the reader, the teacher coaches her by reading along with her.

Teacher: Okay, Theresa, now I want you to try reading that same section with me. Make sure you change your voice when Cherry-Sue is talking, just like I did. Think about how Cherry-Sue would sound in this part.

[Theresa and the teacher read the same lines together, and they change their voices to match the feeling.]

Now the teacher transitions the reader into trying the strategy in her own independent reading book, but continues to support her by reading together.

Teacher: Wow! You really sounded like Cherry-Sue. Now I'd like you to try this same strategy in your own book. Can you turn back to the page in *Minnie and Moo* where you thought Minnie was relaxed? Together, we will read that page in a relaxed voice because you were thinking Minnie is relaxed in that part.

[Theresa and the teacher begin reading together, but Theresa reads in a monotone voice.]

Teacher: Theresa, remember you are trying to sound like Minnie. Make your voice match her feeling.

Theresa: [rereads the first two lines in a soft, relaxed-sounding voice]

Teacher: Keep going, Theresa.

The teacher makes sure to let the reader try the strategy without the support of reading together in order to foster independence.

Theresa: [continues to the end of the page without the teacher]

Teacher: Theresa, I hope you always remember to make your voice match the character's feelings when you read. You can do this when you read aloud or when you read in your head. Our voice should match the character's feelings whenever we read so that we better understand the characters in our books.

At the end of the conference, the teacher restates the strategy and reminds the reader to continue using it from now on.

Supporting Students in Whole-Class Studies

Method: Coaching

In this conference, the teacher begins by researching one of the whole-class study goals.

Teacher: Hi Tony! Can you please take a book out of your baggie that has some challenging words in it?

Tony, a first-grader: [looks through his bag of books and chooses one called *Grandpa*, by Jillian Cutting]

Teacher: I'd like to listen to you read this book.

Tony: [looks at the cover and reads] "Grandpa." [Then he turns to the first page and reads] "I like to go out with my grandfather [but the book says, 'grandpa']. We have fun together." [He turns to the next page and reads] "We go to the field [but the book says, 'park']. We take a bat and balls."

The teacher compliments the reader on what he is just learning to do as a reader.

Teacher: Tony, you can stop now. I am so impressed that when you were reading you made sure what you said made sense. Readers always make sure the words they say make sense and match the picture, just like yours did.

Tony: [smiles]

The teacher begins coaching the reader to read with more accuracy in his own independent reading book. She first names what she wants him to do.

Teacher: I'd like you to go back to the first page you read and make sure every word you read makes sense and looks right.

Tony: [starts reading] "I like to go out with my grandpa. We have fun together." [He continues] "We go to the field."

Teacher: Does that look right? Look at the first few letters.

Tony: No, it can't be *field* because there is no *f.* We go to the p-park.

Teacher: Does that make sense?

Tony: Yep.

Teacher: I like how you looked closely at the beginning letters of the word and made sure it looked right when you said the word "park."

Tony: [continues reading] "We take a bat and ball."

Teacher: Look closely at the ending letters.

Tony: Oops. "We take a bat and balls."

Teacher: Good job looking closely at the ending of that word to make sure it looked right.

The teacher coaches the reader with generalizable prompts. The teacher also reinforces the reader's strategy by naming it and complimenting as he reads.

Teacher: I like the way you reread these pages and made sure that all the words made sense and looked right. When they didn't look right, like when you said "field" instead of "park," you fixed it. Please remember to always make sure the words you read make sense and look right and if they don't, to fix them.

The teacher remembered to restate the strategy she coached in a way that makes it generalizable to all reading experiences.

Group Conferring

Method: Demonstration

Teacher: Hey group. I pulled you all together today because when I worked with you in a conference this week, I noticed that you all picked nonfiction books on topics that were kind of new to you. You seem so into these cool topics—skeletons, desert animals, volcanoes, ostriches—that I want to help you read them even better. One of the things you're going to have to do in these books, since they're on topics you don't already know too much about, is to figure out new, tricky words. Now, I have no doubt that you'll all be able to *read* the words when you get to them, but I'm not sure you'll always know what they mean right away. Have you noticed this in your books already?

The teacher began by telling the readers why she pulled them over for a group conference and connected the strategy she is teaching to their current books.

Samantha: Yeah. I found two words just on the page I was reading today.

Teacher: And what did you do?

Samantha: I just kept on reading.

Teacher: I can teach you a strategy so you don't have to just skip the word. Have other people done the same thing as Sam—just kept on going when you got to a word you didn't know?

[The readers all nod their heads.]

Teacher: I want you to spy on me as I show you what I do when I come to a new word. I'm going to read this book about volcanoes. I don't know too much about volcanoes, and I bet when I read I'm going to get to a word I don't know. I want you to watch carefully to see how I read the sentence that the word is in, and the sentence after to help me to figure out what the new word means. Once I think I know the meaning, I'm going to go back to the sentence and stick that meaning in the sentence to see if it makes sense.

The teacher made sure to set up the readers for what strategy to observe in the demonstration that follows.

Teacher: [reads] "Volcanos, earthquakes, tidal waves, hurricanes, flash floods, and forest fires—nature running wild is both spectacular and terrifying." Okay, I'm okay so far. I knew all of those words. The sentence made sense.

Teacher: [reads] "Despite all our modern resources, natural disasters still devastate lives." Hmm. "Devastate." I don't know that word. Let me reread the sentence. "Despite all our modern resources, natural disasters still devastate lives." Okay, that didn't help. Let me read on to see if the next sentence helps me.

Teacher: [reads] "Every year, they kill, injure, or leave homeless millions of people." Hmm. Okay, I think I know what *devastate* might mean. I think that examples of devastating are killing and injuring and leaving people homeless. So I think *devastate* might mean to make your life terrible. Let me stick that definition back into the sentence to see if it makes sense. "Despite all our modern resources, natural disasters still *make your life terrible*." Yup. That makes sense! Now I can keep going.

So did you notice when I got to a hard word, I used the sentence that the word is in, and the sentence after the word to help me out? I thought about what the word might mean, and then I went back and tried the word in my sentence. Tell your partner what you saw.

Samantha and Jonathon:

Samantha: She did a lot of rereading.

Jonathon: Yeah, I noticed that. She didn't keep going like we did!

Samantha: Yeah. She also looked in the sentence where the tricky word was and when she didn't find the meaning, she looked in the next sentence.

Thea: I noticed that she looked in the sentence that has the word and the sentence after and was able to figure it out.

Jack: And when she had an idea about what the word meant, she went back and stuck it in the sentence to double-check.

Teacher: Okay, let's make a list of steps for what you can do when you get to a tricky word:

[The teacher makes a chart]

1. Reread the sentence that has the word, and the sentence after that one to look for clues.

2. Think about what the word could mean based on what you read.

3. Go back and try the definition of what you think it means in the sentence to see if it makes sense.

Teacher: Are you ready to try it in your books?

[Every student starts reading in his or her own book.]

After the demonstration the teacher makes sure she coaches every reader using the new strategy.

[The teacher listens to one of the readers, Thea.]

Thea: [reads] "Ostriches can run faster than the fastest human sprinter." Hmm. I don't know that word—*sprinter*.

Teacher: So what can you do?

Thea: I'm going to read to see if I learn more in the next sentence.

Teacher: Good.

Thea: [reads] "They can run as fast as forty miles per hour." Um, I think a *sprinter* is a runner.

Teacher: What makes you think that?

Thea: Well, both of these sentences talk about running.

Teacher: Stick the word *runner* back in the sentence to see if it makes sense.

[The teacher moves to listen to another reader.]

Jack: I found a word I don't know. It's *ligament*.

Teacher: Show me where you found that word.

Jack: Right here. There aren't any sentences after this sentence, but the sentence before says "Strong, stretchy bands, called rubber bands, are what hold the bones together." I think that a *ligament* is a strong, stretchy band because the word *ligament* is in a sentence that says "These are ligaments."

Teacher: Can I interrupt all of you for a moment? Jack just discovered something so important! He found a place in his book where the definition is *before* the word. A whole sentence before! So let's add that to our chart, and be on the lookout for that in other books!

[The teacher listens and coaches the last two students.]

Teacher: Okay, everyone. So now you know something very powerful. You know that when you get to a new word—in your nonfiction books, or anytime—you have a strategy to help you out. You know you can:

1. Reread the sentence that has the word, the sentence after that one, *or the sentence before that one* to look for clues.

2. Think about what the word could mean based on what you read.

3. Go back and try the definition of what you think it means in the sentence to see if it makes sense.

The teacher made a chart in this conference to leave a concrete example of the steps of the strategy. Readers can reference the chart as needed.

Teacher: Remember to keep using this strategy from now on.

Bibliography

ADLER, DAVID A. 1997. *Cam Jansen and the Mystery of the U.F.O.* New York: Puffin Books.

ALLINGTON, RICHARD L. 2001. *What Really Matters for Struggling Readers: Designing Research-Based Programs.* New York: Addison-Wesley Educational Publishers, Inc.

ANDERSON, CARL. 2005. *Assessing Writers.* Portsmouth, NH: Heinemann.

——. 2000. *How's it going?* Portsmouth, NH: Heinemann.

ANGELILLO, JANET. 2003. *Writing About Reading: From Book Talk to Literary Essays, Grades 3–8.* Portsmouth, NH: Heinemann.

BAUM, L. 1900. *The Wonderful Wizard of Oz.* New York: Dover Publications.

BEERS, KYLENE. 2003. *When Kids Can't Read, What Teachers Can Do.* Portsmouth, NH: Heinemann.

CALKINS, LUCY. 2001. *The Art of Teaching Reading.* New York: Longman.

——. 1986. *The Art of Teaching Writing.* Portsmouth, NH: Heinemann.

CALKINS, LUCY, AND THE TEACHERS COLLEGE READING AND WRITING PROJECT COMMUNITY. 2002. *A Field Guide to the Classroom Library.* Portsmouth, NH: Heinemann.

CALKINS, LUCY, MARY CHIARELLA, KATHY COLLINS, M. COLLEEN CRUZ, CORY GILLETTE, TED KESSLER, MAJORIE MARTINELLI, MADEA McEVOY. 2006. *Units of Study for Teaching Writing: Grades 3–5.* Portsmouth, NH: Heinemann.

CALKINS, LUCY, PAT BLEICHMAN, AMANDA HARTMAN, NATIALIE LOUS, LEAH MERMELSTEIN, ABBY OXENHORN, LAURIE PESSAH, AND STEPHANIE PARSONS. 2003. *Units of Study in Primary Writing: A Yearlong Curriculum.* Portsmouth, NH: Heinemann.

CALKINS, LUCY, AMANDA HARTMAN, AND ZOE WHITE. 2005. *One to One.* Portsmouth, NH: Heinemann.

CAMBOURNE, BRIAN. 1988. *The Whole Story: Natural Learning and the Acquisition of Literacy in the Classroom.* New Zealand: Aston Scholastic Limited.

CAMERON, ANN. 1989. *Stories Julian Tells.* New York: Knopf Publishing Group.

CAZET, DENYS. 1998. *Minnie and Moo Go Dancing.* New York: DK Publishing, Inc.

CHARLOTTE'S WEB. 1976. Produced by Joseph Barbara and William Hana. Directed by Charles A. Nichols and Iwao Takamoto. 94 minutes. Paramount Pictures. Film.

CLAY, MARIE. 2000. *Running Records for Classroom Teachers.* Portsmouth, NH: Heinemann.

COLE, ARDITH DAVIS. 2003. *Knee to Knee, Eye to Eye: Circling in on Comprehension.* Portsmouth, NH: Heinemann.

COLLINS, KATHY. 2004. *Growing Readers.* Portland, ME: Stenhouse.

CRUZ, COLLEEN. 2004. *Independent Writing: One Teacher—32 Needs, Topics, and Plans.* Portsmouth, NH: Heinemann.

CUTTING, JILLIAN. 1990. *Grandpa.* Chicago, IL: The Wright Group.

DAHL, ROALD. 1964. *Charlie and the Chocolate Factory.* New York, NY: Penguin Books.

FIELDING, LINDA, AND DAVID PEARSON. 1994. "Reading Comprehension: What Works?" *Educational Leadership* 51(5): 62–67.

FOUNTAS, IRENE C., AND GAY SU PINNELL. 2001. *Guiding Readers and Writers: Teaching Comprehension, Genre, and Content Literacy.* Portsmouth, NH: Heinemann.

———. 1996. *Guided Reading: Good First Teaching for All Children.* Portsmouth, NH: Heinemann.

———. 1999. *Matching Books to Readers: Using Leveled Books in Guided Reading, K–3.*

Portsmouth, NH: Heinemann.

———. 2005. *Leveled Books K–8.* Portsmouth, NH: Heinemann.

GRIFFEY, HARRIET. 1998. *Volcanoes and Other Natural Disasters.* New York: DK Publishing, Inc.

HARVEY, STEPHANIE, AND ANNE GOUDVIS. 2000. *Strategies That Work.* Portland, ME: Stenhouse.

HENKES, KEVIN. 1990. *Julius the Baby of the World.* New York: Greenwillow Books.

KEENE, ELLIN OLIVER, AND SUSAN ZIMMERMANN. 1997. *Mosaic of Thought: Teaching Comprehension in a Reader's Workshop.* Portsmouth, NH: Heinemann.

KLINE, SUZY. 1997. *Horrible Harry in Room 2B.* New York: Puffin Books.

MARSHALL, EDWARD. 1982. *Fox and Friends.* New York: Puffin Books.

MCDONALD, MEGAN. 2004. *Judy Moody Saves the World.* New York: Candlewick Press.

MILNE, A.A. 1988. *Winnie the Pooh.* New York: Penguin Young Readers Group.

NATIONAL ENDOWMENT FOR THE ARTS. 2004. *Reading at Risk: A Survey of Literary Reading in America. http://www.nea.gov/news/news04/ReadingAtRisk.html.*

PATERSON, KATHERINE. 1977. *Bridge to Terabithia.* New York: Harper Trophy.

PETERSON, BARBARA. 2001. *Literary Pathways: Selecting Books to Support New Readers.* Portsmouth, NH: Heinemann.

RANSOM, CANDICE. 2002. *Goldilocks and the Three Bears.* San Francisco, CA: Brighter Child Series.

RYLANT, CYNTHIA. 1987. *Henry and Mudge: The First Book.* New York: Aladdin Books.

———. 2002. *Mr. Putter and Tabby Catch the Cold.* San Diego: Harcourt, Inc.

———. 1994a. *Mr. Putter and Tabby Pour the Tea.* San Diego: Harcourt, Inc.

———. 1994b. *Mr. Putter and Tabby Walk the Dog.* San Diego: Harcourt, Inc.

———. 2000. *Poppleton Has Fun.* New York: Scholastic.

SANTMAN, DONNA. 2005. *Shades of Meaning: Comprehension and Interpretation in Middle School.* Portsmouth, NH: Heinemann.

SEUSS, DR., AND JACK PRELUTSKY. 1998. *Hooray for Diffendoofer Day!* New York: Alfred A. Knopf.

SHERMAT, MARJORIE WEINMAN. 1977. *Nate the Great.* New York: Bantam Doubleday Dell Books for Young Readers.